OPAA!

GREEK COOKING NEW YORK STYLE

T0159026

OPAA!

GREEK COOKING NEW YORK STYLE

George J. Gekas

Bonus Books, Inc., Chicago

01 00 99 98 97   5 4 3 2 1

Library of Congress Cataloging-in-Publication Data

Gekas, George J.
    Opaa!: Greek cooking New York style / George J. Gekas.
      p.   cm.
    Includes index.
    ISBN 1-56625-078-1 (pbk.)
    1. Cookery, Greek.   2. Cookery—New York (State)—New York.
I. Title.
TX723.5.G8G41824 1997
641.59495—dc21   96-37410

Bonus Books, Inc.
160 East Illinois Street
Chicago, Illinois 60611

Composition by Point West, Inc.

Printed in the United States of America

Contents

Acknowledgments

I would like to thank those who contributed, tested, and proofread the recipes in this book. Their diligence and commitment have assured excellent recipes.

Special thanks to Mary Pappas, for her extensive research on familiar quotations on cookery. Many thanks to Elaine Bozikas, who helped me with her Greek translation of many recipes. A special thanks to my wife, Helen, who assisted me in the preparation of many recipes.*

Contributors:

Bertha Capulos
Bertha Dangles
James Gekas
Connie Gekas
Mom Gekas
Helen Gekas
Marion Gekas
Olga Gekas
Thomas Gekas
Emily Gyann

Mary Pappas
Georgette Kontos
Nick Panos
Demetra Pappas
Vasiliki Pappas
Stella Pavlatos
Sam Tolia
Canella Woyar
Mark Woyar

*Thanks to Sam Tolia for the wonderful illustrations and cover design. Special thanks to Peter S. Makrias, publisher and editor of *Estiator—The Restaurateur*, the national magazine of the Greek–American food industry, for his professional advice.

Introduction:
Your Passport to New York Greeks

Who says Greeks can't cook? What is "Greek cuisine"? Is there a style of cooking which is truly Greek, in other words, ways of cooking which have not been borrowed from neighboring countries, such as Turkey and Italy? Although many so-called experts have crossed out Greek cuisine from their lists, I ask, is that right?

We Greeks in the field of gastronomy say "no!" On the contrary, Greek cuisine is one of the most superb cuisines and is based on the most ancient traditions in the world. Greek cuisine is more than 25 centuries old. It is the first European cuisine both in tradition and quality. When the uncivilized inhabitants of Europe knew nothing about cuisine except "roast meat," in that ancient land 2,500 years ago—even before the classical "Golden Age of Greece"—our ancestors knew how to mix and combine various ingredients and spices to make food tasty and satisfying to the palate, a fact verified by both Greek and foreign historians and archaeologists.

During the earliest years of our history, even writers and philosophers did not hesitate to try new combinations, create delectable dishes and sweetmeats, and record the recipes in special cookbooks, the first of their kind.

Greece has contributed many writers to the field of gastronomy who created and praised the beauties of Greek recipes. But, unfortunately, their works were lost along with other masterpieces in the disastrous fire which destroyed the library of Alexandria during the 7th century A.D.

Admittedly, the history of Greek cuisine does not begin with Homer. Then, roast meat was still the primary way of cooking. However, since the archaic period—2 centuries before the classic age—Greek cooking technique began to develop and bloom. During this time, Greeks were uppermost in devising combinations of vegetables cooked with meat, which produced a special flavor unknown to man.

Bread was a specialty of the ancient Athenians. White and flavorful ever since Theorion, a Greek from Sicily, perfected the process of its preparation, the bread was as good as any made today.

But it was during the time of Alexander the Great that Greek cooking really progressed to an art.

The climate and geography of Greece have always been major influences on its people's cuisine. The juicy lemons, tangy olives, and fresh herbs and vegetables that grow in Greece's warm sunshine are some of the country's best-loved foods.

Fishing is a major industry in Greece. Not surprisingly, Greeks enjoy many seafood dishes. One simple recipe uses only oregano—a very popular Greek herb—and fresh lemon juice for flavoring.

Lamb is the most popular meat in Greece, though chicken, pork, and beef are enjoyed as well. Olive trees grow all over in Greece, supplying olive oil for cooking, salads, and flavoring foods.

Honey, which is found wild in all parts of Greece, is the Greek's favorite sweetener. Many of the very sweet pastries Greeks enjoy are sweetened with honey.

The French actually did not learn how to cook until the beginning of the 17th century, and they are not embarrassed to admit it. It was the Greeks who taught the Romans how to cook, and the Romans who taught the French. But regardless of the influence Greek cooking has had on other national cuisines, we are not looking for credit or applause. All we want is for Greek cuisine to survive. With the help of this cookbook, we'll get our wish and you'll get many enjoyable meals.

Greek-English Glossary

Arni—Lamb.

Farina—Cream of wheat.

Feta—The Greek cheese best known in America, and it is the most popular native cheese in Greece. Soft and very salty, it is usually made from goat's milk.

Fide (fidelo)—A very fine egg noodle. Sold in the U.S. as fidelo, fidilini, etc.

Floyeres—Phyllo pastry having a long, flute-like shape.

Fasolatha—Meatless bean soup.

Fasoulakia—Green or string beans.

Fournou—Baked.

Galatoboureko—A baked custard dessert with thin pastry sheets on top and bottom and syrup spread all over.

Galopoula—Turkey.

Grapevine leaves—Used for preparing dolmathes. Are soaked in brine and used to make stuffed grape leaves. They are sold in supermarkets and Greek or Middle Eastern grocery stores.

Garides—Shrimp.

Halvah—Comes from a Turkish word that means "sweet meat." Homemade halvah is nothing like the commercial sesame-seed confection. You must try it to really understand it.

Iman Baildi—This dish is so delicious, a real treat of eggplant and trimmings. Legend has it that Iman (high priest) fainted in delight when served this.

Kasseri—A hard, yellow-white table cheese, rich in a flavor all its own. Hard rind should be removed before using. You may substitute parmesan or romano cheese—both these cheeses have a stronger flavor. Sold in Greek and Italian grocery stores.

Kafes—Coffee.

Kalamaria—Squid.

Kanelata—With cinnamon.

Karithata—A short cookie with nuts.

Keftedes—Meatballs.

Patates—Potatoes.

Paximadia—Biscuits served with a hot beverage.

Phyllo (filo)—Pronounced "fee-low," it's a tissue-thin, buttery dough made from flour and water. To make it takes great skill. This thin dough is actually pulled, not rolled. You will wind up making holes if you roll it. Phyllo is available in supermarkets and Greek, Italian, and Lebanese grocery stores. Phyllo comes in a one-pound box with 20 to 29 sheets. Just in case your recipe calls for $1/2$ pound, you can save the remainder by wrapping the unused $1/2$ pound in waxed paper and refrigerate. Good for 4 weeks or more. An unopened box may be stored for several months by freezing.

Pignolias—Used in various desserts and stuffings, also called pine nuts.

Pilafi—Rice, boiled with meat, poultry, or other stock.

Psari—Fish.

Renga—Smoked herring.

Rizi—Raw rice.

Rizogalo—Rice pudding.

Salata—Salad.

Saltsa—Sauce.

Skaras—Broiled.

Soupa—Soup.

Salted cod—Fish favorite for many dishes.

Souvlakia—Shish kebab.

Skordalia—Greek folks' favorite garlic sauce. Very strong—powerful.

Spanakorizo—Spinach rice pilaf.

Spanakopeta—Spinach pie made with phyllo.

Tarama—Carp roe.

Tiropetakia—Cheese puffs made with phyllo, shaped in triangles, and baked till crisp and golden brown.

Trahana—A homemade noodle used in soups and meat stews. Semolina is a good substitute if trahana is unobtainable.

Vissino—Sour cherries in a delicious preserve.

Yaourti—Yogurt. Delicious plain. Used over pilafi.

Greek Spices, Herbs, and Flavorings

All Greek herbs and flavorings originated in the Mediterranean and have gradually found their way to the United States. Greek cooks began to enhance food with these exotic flavors. You will enjoy experimenting with traditional herbs and spices to flavor your favorite recipes.

Anise Seed (Glikaniso)
The licorice flavor comes from the seeds of the green plants of the parsley family. This spice is added to cakes, pastries, and sweet breads.

Basil (Vasilikos)
The seeds of this plant give a distinct flavor to soups, stews, and salads.

Bay Leaf (Dafni)
The leaf of the sweet bay tree has a flavor that goes with stews, fish, and meat.

Cinnamon (Kanella)
Common in many Greek recipes. Used most often in a powder form.

Coriander (Koliantro)
This aromatic seed is used to spice meats, pastries, and cheese.

Cumin (Kimino)
The Greek people from Smyrna used this spice to flavor meats.

Dill (Anithon)
Dill seeds are similar to fresh fennel. Used to flavor soups, fresh dill is a great addition to a tossed salad.

Fennel (Anithos)
This plant adds a sweet licorice flavor to soups, stews, and vegetables. Seeds are used in cookies and cakes.

Garlic (Skordo)
Only a few recipes call for this herb, and the Greeks use it sparingly. Buy by the bulb and don't refrigerate.

Ginger, Fresh (Zigivero)
This spice was always hard to get, which limited its use in recipes. Keep refrigerated—uncovered and unwrapped.

Lemon (Lemoni)
The lemon is the most important fruit flavoring in Greek cooking. It is the secret ingredient in the syrup for Greek desserts, and it is also used to flavor fish, meat, and fowl. Don't forget the egg and lemon sauce.

Mahaleb (Mahlepi)
The seeds are used in holiday breads and cakes.

Marjoram (Matzourana)
Used as frequently as basil or oregano to flavor fish or stews.

Mastic (Mastiha)
This unusual Greek flavoring grows only on the island of Chios. The resin, tapped from the lentisk bush, makes a delicious chewing gum. It is also used in liqueurs, drinks, cakes, candies, and cookies.

Mint (Thiosmos)
The mint used in most Greek cooking is the spearmint, also used to flavor candy. For Greek cooking it's used in vegetables, lamb, beef, and salads.

Mustard Seed (Moustrarda Sinapi)
Mustard seed was called silphium by ancient Greeks, and sprinkled like pepper over vegetables, meat, and fish.

Nutmeg (Moshokarido)
The Greeks call this the sweet-smelling nut. It is ground to a powder for desserts, drinks, cakes, and cookies.

Oregano (Oregano)
Without the flavor of oregano on pork, fowl, lamb, or beef, a Greek would not consider the meat properly prepared.

Parsley (Maintanos)
Both the open growing and the dense leaved parsley, described by Heophrastus in the 4th century B.C., were introduced to America in the 17th century. Greek cooks use it generously in their foods.

Pepper (Piperi)
Pepper was one of the first spices to be introduced into Greece from the Indian Archipelago. It was so expensive that myrtle berries, now called Jamaican pepper, were used in its place.

Rose (Triantafillo)
The strong yet delicate flavoring of rose is used primarily to flavor desserts, syrups, and candies.

Rosemary (Dendrolivano)
This herb comes from a sweet-smelling bush with tiny, needle-like leaves and is used to flavor meat, fish, and sauces.

Sage (Faskomilia)
Sweet-smelling sage is used to flavor pork, poultry, and stuffings.

Salt (Alati)
Salt evaporated from the sea was the first kind the early Greeks knew and used. Greek cooks in restaurants prefer using liberal amounts of salt. My advice is to test your food before adding salt.

Savory (Thrumbi)
Savory is an herb similar to sage and goes well sprinkled over pork and poultry.

Sesame (Sesame)
Sesame seeds, grown on the island of Kos, have a nutlike flavor and are used as topping for breads and sweet cookies.

Thyme (Themari)
This dry leaf lends its pungent flavor to fish, fowl, and most importantly, to lamb.

Vinegar (Ksidi)
The vinegar used in Greek cuisine is naturally a wine vinegar. It's used liberally in cooking and over salads.

"Joy, temperance, and repose, slam the door on the doctor's nose."

Longfellow

"Health is the soul that animates all the enjoyments of life, which fade and are tasteless without it."

Sir W. Temple

"Go to your banquet, then, but use delight,
So as to rise still with an appetite."

Herrick

"They are as sick that surfeit with too much, as they that starve with nothing."

Shakespeare

Keeping Food Fresh

Assuming the food you have bought is fresh, it's how you take care of it after leaving the store that determines your safety. Two million cases of food poisoning are caused each day by improper food handling in the home. So here are some general guidelines for storing as well as specific ones for staples, bread and baking supplies, fruits and vegetables, dairy products, meats, and fish.

Begin by paying attention to product labeling. "Sell by" and "pull" dates let the consumer know the last day a product can be sold. In general, milk and cream products stay unspoiled 7 days after the "sell by" date.

Do not store canned foods for 2 to 3 years and expect them to retain their fresh flavor upon opening. If the cans are not dented, leaking, or rusting, the shelf life for high-acid foods such as juices, fruits, pickles, and vinegar-based dishes is about 1 year. While they might still be technically safe to eat after that, the nutrients and flavor begin to decline. Store canned goods at temperatures below 85 degrees, except for canned hams, which should be refrigerated and used within 6 to 9 months.

The key to safe refrigerated and frozen products is correct temperature setting. The refrigerator section should stay between 34° and 40°. (A thermometer will alert you to temperature fluctuations.) The freezer should be kept at about 0° and should never rise above 5°.

It is recommended when packaging items for the freezer (especially meat and poultry) that you throw away the product's original wrap and use vapor-proof paper, plastic freezer wrap, or a freezer container. Date the food as you freeze it, and place it in the rear of the freezer so that you will use the older items in the front first.

Staples

Keep oils in a cool, dark place for a minimum shelf life of 1 year. According to Robert Reeves of the Institute of Shortening and Edible Oils, "The state of refinement in today's oils makes it so that they don't require refrigeration, and the bottom line is that it's taking up extra space in your refrigerator."

Store opened packages of pasta in a sealed plastic bag (to avoid bugs) in a cool dark place. Whole wheat pasta becomes rancid very quickly because of the oil in the kernel and should be stored in the refrigerator (bring to room temperature before cooking).

Do not refrigerate chocolate—the drop in temperature causes the cocoa butter to rise to the surface of the chocolate, creating an off-white bloom, which, while unsightly, doesn't actually harm the chocolate. Instead, wrap and keep it in a cool, dry, dark place.

Store shelled nuts in a covered jar in the refrigerator; store loose unshelled nuts in a plastic bag in the refrigerator.

For fresh tasting coffee, store beans, wrapped air tight, in the freezer. A large economy-size can of coffee is no bargain if you don't use it within a week or so after opening.

Fruits and Vegetables

Vegetables are harvested at the peak of their flavor and should be kept in the refrigerator to retard any overripening. Fruit, on the other hand, is usually harvested while unripe, and should ripen at room temperature for a few days until ready to serve (exceptions are apples, cherries, grapes, and berries, which are usually ripe at time of purchase and should be refrigerated). And watch out for tropical fruits, tomatoes, and yams; they can't endure temperatures below 50 degrees.

Do not wash fruits and vegetables until just before you use them. The added moisture will hasten bacterial spoilage.

Onions, potatoes, squash, pumpkins, waxed rutabagas, and whole uncut watermelons should be stored in a cool, well-ventilated area, away from dishwashers, stoves, and refrigerators, which give off heat.

Store garlic in a cool, dark spot. Ginger should be kept in a covered glass jar in the refrigerator.

Refrigerate fresh herbs, with stems intact, in a covered jar with one inch of water. Or wrap the stem ends with a damp paper towel and place the herbs in a ventilated plastic bag. Do not wash herbs until you use them.

To save herbs for longer periods of time, try making herb vinegar. Place whole sprigs or leaves of herbs in clean glass bottles with nonmetallic tops. Cover them with a good vinegar, label, and store the capped bottles for at least a month before using.

Fresh herbs can also be dried for longer storage. Place fresh herbs in a single layer on a baking sheet in a preheated 200° oven until dry. The dried herbs should then be stored in glass containers in a cool, dark place. Dried herbs should be replaced every 3 to 6 months. Avoid dried herbs and spices sold in cellophane packages or bottles with cork stoppers—they let the air in.

Meat

Meat, according to Andy Zimmerman, owner of several meat markets, should be rewrapped at home in plastic wrap (not foil because that turns the meat dark) and put in the chilliest section of the refrigerator. You can store meat there up to 4 days. A slightly brown color does not automatically signal spoilage. The blood travels down through the meat while it sits, and to preserve the blood-red color, you must turn it over occasionally.

Zimmerman advises against freezing meats. He says it changes the texture and complexity of the meat—the better the cut of meat, the less you want to freeze it, as the change will be all the more marked. If you must freeze the meat, be sure to wrap it in freezer paper very tightly and keep it in the freezer no longer than 6 to 9 months, tops.

How to tell if your steak has gone bad? First off, you can smell the rancid odor a mile away. To confirm that this is coming from the steak and not something it might have come in contact with, he suggests trying to wash it off. If the steak looks old, dried out, or if the color has changed dramatically, it's time for it to go. "And, simply, if it feels slimy and greasy, you know this is something you don't want to put in your mouth."

The same rules apply to lamb, veal, and pork.

Poultry, of course, does not hold up as long as meat. One to 2 days in the refrigerator and 3 to 4 months in the freezer is the maximum. Each piece should be rewrapped individually in plastic wrap or freezer paper. Smell and slimy texture are primary indicators that poultry has gone bad.

Luncheon meats can be stored unopened in the refrigerator for 2 weeks. Opened, they can last 3 to 5 days if the package has been rewrapped well after using.

Dairy

All cheeses should be kept tightly wrapped. Air is the enemy. I suggest a double piece of foil, but not plastic, as it tends to impart a flavor. If you do use a plastic it should be of good quality and stretchable to create a tight seal.

Whether it should be refrigerated depends on the cheese. The longer you want to hold it, of course, the more crucial it is that you lower the temperature. But this idea of storing cheese is a recent invention. You should leave the cheese intact until you are ready to serve it. Forty years ago you went to the cheese store, bought your cheese, served it, and finished it in one sitting.

If a cheese starts to dry out, unwrap the cheese and rewrap it in a damp paper towel, covering with foil again and leaving it for 24 hours in the refrigerator. I oppose freezing cheese. It's an act of murder. When you freeze cheese, you freeze it permanently. It might be brought back to room temperature, but it will not continue to ripen.

Butter should be stored in the refrigerator, tightly wrapped so it won't absorb odors.

For best quality, keep whole eggs and hard-boiled eggs refrigerated and use within the week of purchase (the longest is 5 weeks). It's best not to keep the eggs in the egg compartment: the repeated temperature fluctuation and slamming of the door deteriorates them.

Fish

If you're going to eat fish the same day you bought it, you can keep it in the same bag in the refrigerator until cooking time. If you want to save it longer, take it out of the original paper and wrap it in plastic wrap, so it won't stick as it dries out, and place it in the refrigerator.

It should be safe there for 3 days. You need nothing but your nose to tell you a piece of fish has gone bad. "It's not a bad odor like scallops; they have a particular odor of their own. In most cases, it's an ammonia smell."

Clams, oysters, and mussels have a storage life of 3 to 4 days, but you must keep their shells moist. The easiest way: Refrigerate them in a plastic bag with holes poked through or in a large bowl with a bit of ice to drip down.

Bread and Baking Supplies

Bread, says Erwin Burlimann, executive chef at Bread and Chocolate Bakery, should never be kept in the refrigerator. It collects moisture and becomes soggy; better to freeze it and slice as needed.

Delicate breads like French and Italian, he says, should be placed in sealable bags to keep them from drying out, or frozen if you plan to heat it. To crisp the outside of the bread, place in a 75° oven for 2 to 3 minutes. Once thawed and reheated, however, the bread must be consumed at that sitting or thrown away—it would be too dry if left over.

A heartier bread, like a six-grain bread, can be cut in half—one half for the freezer, the other for the table. It can handle more moisture and thus doesn't have to be reheated when thawed.

An opened can of baking powder or soda should stay fresh for about 6 months, unrefrigerated. To determine whether your baking powder is fresh, pour 1/4 cup hot water over 1/2 teaspoon of baking powder. If it doesn't bubble, your bread will not rise.

Store white flour in a tightly sealed glass jar. Whole wheat flour should be stored in the refrigerator because it can become rancid. Remember to bring it back to room temperature, though, as the low temperature will inhibit any yeast growth in bread making.

"The intention of every other piece of prose may be discussed and even mistrusted; but the purpose of a cookery book is one and unmistakable. Its object can conceivably be no other than to increase the happiness of mankind."

Joseph Conrad

"As a lamp is choked by a super abundance of oil, and a fire extinguished by excess of fuel, so is the natural health of the body destroyed by intemperate diet."

Burton

"The greatest animal in creation; the animal who cooks."

Douglas Jerrold

Kitchen Hints

When a recipe calls for finely chopped garlic, onions, or vegetables, these should be finely chopped by hand in order to retain their full flavor. Never put them through a grinder, blender, or masher.

To make sweet cream sour—Add 2 teaspoons lemon juice or 1 teaspoon vinegar to each cup of cream.

To make sweet milk sour—Add 2 tablespoons of lemon juice or vinegar to each cup of sweet milk.

To whip cream readily—Add a few drops of lemon juice and chill thoroughly before whipping.

To keep scalding milk from scorching—Rinse pan with hot water before using.

To clarify fat—Add slices of potato to melted fat and fry until potato is brown. The potato will absorb any foreign flavors and will collect some of the sediment.

Keep salads moist during a buffet with wet paper towels. This works just as well with cold meat.

Stir a pinch of baking soda into milk before boiling it, and the milk will not curdle or form a skin.

A teaspoon of sugar will intensify the taste of a vegetable soup.

A pinch of salt does the same thing for cream or egg whites that are to be whipped.

If soup is too salty, add several slices of raw potato and simmer for a few minutes.

To keep shrimp tender, add them to boiling water and cook only until water returns to a full boil. Drain shrimp immediately and cool them in a bowl placed under cold running water.

To heighten the flavor of corn, add the tender inside green husks to the cooking water.

You can magically neutralize the smell given off by vegetables in the cabbage family by adding two bay leaves in the cooking water.

To keep filling from soaking through a prebaked pie crust, brush the inner surface of the crust with slightly beaten egg white, and let the coating dry briefly before adding the filling.

Check fish for freshness—the eyes should be clean and bulging, bright and shiny. The gills should be checked to see that they are clean looking, not pale looking.

Kitchen Hints (continued)

To hard boil egg yolks—Drop into simmering water and keep below boiling until firm.

To hold eggs together while poaching—Add a few drops of vinegar or lemon juice to the cooking water.

Doubt the freshness of your eggs? Test by placing in a deep bowl of water. The eggs staying on the bottom are okay, the floaters get pitched.

To keep egg yolk from adhering to pans and dishes, do not wash them in hot water. Instead, place dishes or pans in cold water. Or run cold water over it as soon as possible. Then wash it in soapy hot water.

Never use milk in an omelette. Use only water. Milk makes your omelette watery since it will not blend with the eggs. Water blends and helps keep the omelette high.

The basic rules for good omelettes—Use butter and peanut oil in your cooking. The blend of the two will prevent the butter from burning and will give the eggs fine flavor and color.

For good quiche, precook the pastry shell. This prevents that soggy bottom.

Remove unnecessary moisture from vegetables by cooking them a bit before placing them in egg mixture.

Have your eggs at room temperature to enhance blending.

Heat your pan before you put in the peanut oil and butter. When the butter stops foaming, add your eggs.

Peel onions under water to keep from affecting eyes.

To skin a tomato easily, place a fork through the stem end, plunge into boiling water and then into cold water.

To help spinach retain its color—Add lemon juice while cooking.

To keep fresh parsley, mint, and watercress, wash thoroughly, shake off excess water, place in glass jar, cover, and place in refrigerator.

To separate lettuce leaves easily—Cut out core and place lettuce head under running cold water so that it enters into the cavity.

To keep cauliflower white—Add fresh lemon to cauliflower while cooking.

In eggplant dishes, use small rather than large eggplants.

Cut, chop, or mince vegetables on a terrycloth. They will not slip around as they tend to do on a hard surface and your workboard is kept clean.

Kitchen Hints (continued)

Never let raw poultry, or its juices, come in contact with any other raw or cooked food.

Always use a clean towel or rag—or paper towels—to clean kitchen surfaces after you work with chicken. Wash cutting boards, knives, and the counter with detergent and hot water immediately after cutting up the raw chicken.

Use a clean acrylic cutting board; save the wooden ones for cutting only bread and raw vegetables.

Serve cooked poultry on clean plates. Never put grilled chicken back on the plate with raw juices.

Cook chicken immediately after thawing. And never interrupt the cooking process.

With leftovers, reheat to an internal temperature of 165 degrees and let sauces and gravies reach the boiling point.

Refrigerate chicken as soon as possible after you buy it.

Always thaw frozen poultry in the refrigerator or, if you're in a hurry, in a bag under cold running water. Never thaw it on the kitchen counter.

Finally, when in doubt, throw it out.

I use two kinds of oil in our kitchen. I prefer peanut oil for frying of any kind since it will withstand high temperatures without burning. Olive oil is my other choice—it's great for Greek cooking, especially when you want rich flavor.

Cottage cheese and sour cream will keep longer if the carton is stored upside down in the refrigerator.

A little salt in the frying pan when you are heating oil or other fats for frying will prevent spattering.

A lump of charcoal or a drop of vanilla extract on a piece of cotton placed in the refrigerator prevents unpleasant odors.

Soaking guide—Proper water temperature helps in loosening caked casseroles. Remember to soak sugared messes in hot water and cheese and egg crusts in cold water.

Vegetables should be the freshest you can get. Never overcook them; it is better to undercook. Don't let them stand after you've picked them from your garden, or taken them from refrigerator. Cook them immediately or they will lose their freshness and may discolor. This light and quick handling makes all the difference in the presentation of your finished vegetable dish.

Kitchen Hints (continued)

Use only fresh seafood, with the exception of dried cod.

After washing, always rub the fish with salt and fresh lemon juice and let it absorb for 30 minutes or more before cooking. This process makes the flesh of the fish more firm.

Whenever possible, use the head, tail, fins, and bones: their use makes for a better flavor, a juicier fish, and a thicker sauce.

To retain as much flavor of the fish as possible, it is best not to use pots, bowls, or containers made of metal.

Equipment
Pots and Pans

Your pots and pans are very important items in the kitchen. Choose good equipment. Here are a few hints to help you in your purchases:

1. Copperware is a good product. It may be initially a higher investment, but it will be well worth it.
2. Stay away from wooden handles. This says that you cannot put the pan in the oven or broiler.
3. Aluminum is a good choice, because it can be cured to prevent sticking, but you must keep it clean and cannot store food in it.
4. Stay away from stainless steel frying pans. You cannot cure them, thus everything will stick. I know that cast iron is very heavy, but if you can manage the weight, it does a good job.
5. Remember this simple rule: Always heat your pan first; add the oil and follow with the food. You will have less sticking.

The Butcher

Good knives are the basic tools of any cook, and good knives are not cheap. But considering all of the gadgets that you don't need, once you know how to use knives properly, a few good ones are a great investment.

Here are a few pointers on the selection and use of knives. First, don't buy a set of knives. There are lots of packaged "complete set of knives" on the market that, at a glance, look as if they would serve every conceivable knife need. Trust me, they do not. These sets are designed more to match than be functional. Buy knives from open stock. There are only 3 basic knives needed in most kitchens—a paring knife, a boning knife, and the one without which no collection of kitchen cutlery is complete: the French chef's knife.

The chef's knife (sometimes called the cook's knife) is the most versatile knife you can own. Once you have learned how to use a chef's knife, you can throw away half a drawer full of kitchen gadgets. It's great for all kinds of mincing, dicing, and slicing chores.

Many inexperienced cooks make the mistake of choosing too small a blade when they select a chef's knife. A good, hefty, well-balanced 8- to 10-inch blade is by far the best choice. With the longer blade, the weight of the knife does most of the work. Make sure that the heel of the chef's knife is deep enough to give you good knuckle clearance when the blade is flush with the cutting board.

When properly used, the chef's knife blade is positioned with the point on the cutting board well beyond the food to be diced, sliced, or chopped. Tuck the knuckles of your free hand under to hold the food and run the flat side of the knife against your fingers, using a rocking motion without lifting the point from the board. This way you can quickly and safely slice, dice, mince, or chop.

The second most important knife in any kitchen is the boning knife. This also comes in a variety of blade sizes, from 4 to 8 inches. My father did the butchering in our restaurant for 60 years using a 6-inch, flexible curve bladed boner. Every time I tried to work with that knife, I'd nick a knuckle. My preference is a 6-inch, straight, stiff, narrow blade. The shape and size is up to you.

Four different styles of paring knives are common: The cook's style, or spear point, which is really just a tiny French chef's knife; and the "curve," "sharp," and "clip" points. Which you choose is purely a matter of personal preference. My favorite is a curve point.

"We may live without poetry, music, and art;
We may live without conscience and live without heart;
We may live without friends, we may live without books;
But civilized man cannot live without cooks."

Owen Meredith

"I am a great eater of beef, and I believe that does harm to my wit."

Shakespeare

APPETIZERS

Fried Smelts (Marithes Tighanites)

- 1 pound smelts (3 to 4 inches long)
- 3/4 cup flour
- 1/2 cup warm water
- 2 tablespoons olive oil
- 1 teaspoon salt
- pinch of white pepper
- 1 egg, beaten
- 1/4 cup olive oil
- 1 lemon, cut in wedges

Wash and clean fish, season with salt and pepper, and set aside. Combine flour and water and stir well until you have a smooth mixture. Add olive oil, salt, and a pinch of pepper. Fold in the beaten egg. The mixture should have the consistency of pancake batter. Dip 2 or 3 fish at a time in batter. Heat olive oil until a drop of water sizzles. Place fish into hot oil and fry until golden brown on both sides.

Place on paper towels to absorb any extra oil. Serve hot with lemon wedges. Makes 10 servings.

Boiled Shrimp (Gharithes Vrastes)

- 2 pounds raw large shrimp
- 1 1/2 cups water
- 2 tablespoons white wine
- 1 carrot, sliced
- 1 onion, sliced
- salt and pepper to taste
- bay leaf
- mayonnaise or olive oil and lemon juice

Wash shrimp in cold water. In a saucepan combine water, wine, carrot, onion, salt, pepper, and bay leaf. Boil 15 minutes. Add shrimp and cook over low heat for 8 minutes. Allow shrimp to cool in the liquid. Drain, shell, and serve coated with mayonnaise or with olive oil and lemon juice. Makes 15 to 20 servings.

Spinach Balls (Spanakokeftedes)

- 3 packages (10 ounces) frozen chopped spinach
- 4 tablespoons butter, melted
- 3 eggs, beaten lightly
- 1 cup grated parmesan cheese
- $1/2$ cup minced dill
- $1/2$ cup feta cheese, crumbled
- salt and pepper to taste
- 1 cup bread crumbs
- vegetable oil for frying

Thaw spinach and drain well. Place spinach and all the remaining ingredients, except bread crumbs, in a medium size bowl. In the palms of your hand, shape the mixture in 1-inch balls. Roll balls in bread crumbs. In a frying pan, heat oil and fry several spinach balls at a time, turning and frying on all sides until golden brown, about 4 to 5 minutes. Drain on paper towel. Serve warm. Makes 30 spinach balls.

Fried Zucchini (Kolokithakia Tiganita)

- 4 small zucchini
- $1/2$ cup all purpose flour
- $1/4$ teaspoon salt
- pinch of pepper
- $1/2$ cup olive oil

Scrub zucchini and wash with cold water. Cut into $1/4$-inch thick slices. Combine flour, salt, and pepper. Gently coat slices on both sides. In a large frying pan, heat oil over medium to high heat. Fry zucchini slices, one layer at a time, until golden brown. Remove cooked zucchini with a spatula or slotted spoon and drain on paper towel.

Great with feta cheese and thin slices of French or crusty bread. Makes 24 servings.

Codfish Caviar Dip (Taramosalata)

Every Greek taverna in Astoria serves taramosalata (Greek caviar). The waiters make you feel that you don't have to be a wealthy person to enjoy it. Try this dip at Roumelis in Astoria.

6 slices Italian bread, crust removed

1 jar (4 ounces) tarama (codfish roe)

juice of 2 lemons

1/4 cup finely grated onion

3/4 cup olive oil

Soak bread in cold water, and squeeze dry. In a blender, blend the bread with tarama until smooth. Keep the blender going and add lemon juice and onion. Still blending, pour in olive oil in a slow, thin stream until mixture has a thick, smooth consistency. Taste for seasoning. If you think it's too salty, add more soaked bread. Refrigerate. Serve with crusty bread or pita bread. A wonderful dip for a first course. Makes 2 cups.

Eggplant Dip (Melitzanosalata)

A delightful appetizer from Greece. The restaurants in New York have been scoring high marks for the past 20 years serving this delightful appetizer. It can also be served as a salad. Spoon mixture onto leaves of lettuce and garnish with parsley and Greek olives.

1 large eggplant

1 onion, thinly sliced

2 cloves garlic, minced

1 tablespoon fresh chopped parsley

1/3 cup olive oil

2 tablespoons red wine vinegar

salt to taste

white pepper to taste

Puncture eggplant with a knife in 3 to 4 places to prevent from exploding while it bakes. Place eggplant in baking dish and bake for 1 hour in a preheated 350° oven. Immerse eggplant in cold water and, using a stainless steel knife to avoid discoloration, cut eggplant in half and remove seeds. Drain excess liquid. Cut into cubes and transfer to a wooden bowl. Add onion, garlic, parsley, olive oil, vinegar, salt, and pepper and mix well. Refrigerate for several hours so flavors may blend. Serve as a spread with crackers and carrot sticks. Yields 2 cups.

Flaming Cheese #1 (Saganaki)

1 egg

$^1/_3$ cup milk

4 ounces kasseri cheese cut in $^1/_2$-inch thick squares

flour

vegetable oil

Beat egg until slightly foaming and light yellow. Add milk, and continue beating. Dip cheese in egg mixture, then in flour (both sides), pressing the cheese so that the flour will stick to the cheese. In a frying pan, heat oil well, so when you place cheese in pan you see a sizzle. Fry cheese on both sides, until golden brown. If you like, splash a few drops of brandy, light it with a match, and shout, "Opaa!" Eat it fast, though, as the pleasure diminishes as it cools off. Makes 1 serving.

NOTE: For best results, make sure your cheese is refrigerated for at least 1 hour before frying. Also, use enough vegetable oil to cover cheese while frying.

Flaming Cheese #2 (Saganaki)

This is a flaming delight that can make a first course. Makes a nice mini-buffet with some calamata Greek olives, sliced tomatoes, crusty bread, lemon wedges, and a glass of hearty wine.
Remember to cook it quickly—you may find yourself a panful of melted cheese, so it's essential that the cheese be kept as cold as possible.

1 pound kasseri or kefalotiri cheese, 4-ounce slices

$^1/_2$ cup flour

1 stick of butter

2 lemons, large wedges

cognac

Place cheese in a bowl, cover with ice water and ice cubes, and refrigerate for an hour until the cheese is very cold. Remove one cheese slice from ice water and pat dry. Flour lightly on both sides. Add two tablespoons of butter to skillet. When butter is sizzling, add the cheese and fry very quickly on both sides. Sprinkle with juice of large lemon wedge, and a few drops of cognac. Ignite and serve as soon as flames die down. Keep on repeating. Makes 4 servings.

Feta Cheese with Herbs

1   tablespoon chopped fresh parsley

1   tablespoon fresh tarragon leaves or
    or $1/2$ teaspoon dried tarragon

1   tablespoon chopped fresh chives

1   scallion, cut in $1/2$-inch pieces

8   ounces cream cheese, cubed (room temperature)

$1/4$ cup whipping cream

$1/4$ pound feta cheese (domestic)

$1/8$ teaspoon white pepper

salt to taste

parsley sprigs

In a food processor combine chopped fresh parsley, tarragon, and chives. Process 30 seconds. Add scallion and process till minced. Remove herb mixture in a small bowl and set aside.

In the food processor combine cream cheese, whipping cream, feta cheese, and pepper. Process until mixture is smooth. Make sure to keep sides scraped. Salt to taste. Return herb mixture to container and process all together for a few seconds until well mixed. Refrigerate 3 to 4 hours or until mixture is thick enough for spreading. Garnish with parsley sprigs. Serve with pita bread or thinly sliced pumpernickel. Serves 12.

Cheese Triangles #1 (Tiropitakia)

$1/2$ pound feta cheese

1   cup grated kefalotiri or parmesan cheese

2   tablespoons finely chopped parsley

2   eggs, beaten

white pepper to taste

$1^1/2$ pounds phyllo sheets (filo)

$1/2$ cup butter, melted for brushing phyllo

Crumble or mash feta cheese with a fork. Add the grated cheese, parsley, eggs, and pepper. Mix well. Cut pastry sheets in strips, about 3 × 12 inches. Stack them one on top of the other and cover with wax paper or cellophane wrap to prevent them from drying out.

Brush each strip with melted butter. Place 1 heaping teaspoon of cheese mixture at one end of the strip. Lift a corner of the strip next to the filling and fold it over the filling so that it touches the opposite long side and forms a triangle enclosing the filling. Continue to fold up the pastry, maintaining the triangular shape. Fill and fold the remaining strips.

Place the puffs in a buttered baking pan and brush lightly with melted butter. Bake in a preheated 350° oven until golden brown, about 20 minutes. Serves 48.

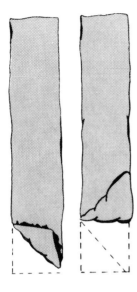

Fold phyllo over filling.
Corner should touch
opposite long side.

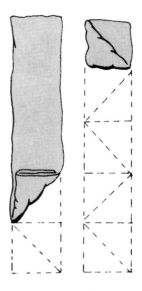

Continue to fold upward,
keeping triangle shape
as shown.

Cheese Triangles #2 (Tiropitakia)

- 4 eggs, well beaten
- 8 ounces cream cheese
- 1 pound feta cheese
- 1 pound phyllo
- ³/₄ pound butter, melted for brushing phyllo

Beat eggs with electric mixer until fluffy. Add cream cheese and continue beating until well blended. Crumble feta cheese with a fork, and combine with egg mixture.
Follow procedures as directed in Triangle 1 recipe. Makes 48.

Cheese Triangles # 3 (Tiropitakia)

- 1 pound feta cheese
- 1 pound small curd cottage cheese
- 4 or 5 eggs
- 1 pound phyllo
- 1/2 pound butter

Crumble feta cheese well, add cottage cheese, and mix well. Add eggs, one at a time, mixing well. The amount of eggs could vary, because of size. Mixture should have a creamy texture.

Follow procedures as directed in Triangle 1 recipe. Makes 40.

NOTE: Cheese puffs may be frozen before baking. Place in a freezer proof container. When ready to bake, brush frozen puffs with melted butter and bake in a preheated 350° oven uncovered for 25 minutes or until golden brown.

Meat Triangles (Bourekakia me Kima)

- 1/4 cup butter
- 1 1/2 pounds lean ground beef
- 1 onion, chopped fine
- 1/2 cup dry white wine
- 2 tomatoes, skinned and chopped
- 1/2 cup water
- 2 tablespoons chopped parsley
- 1 tablespoon dried dill
- 1 teaspoon salt
- pepper to taste
- 1/2 cup parmesan cheese
- 2 tablespoons bread crumbs
- 1 pound phyllo pastry
- 1 cup melted butter, for brushing phyllo

Heat 1/4 cup butter and brown meat. In a small pan saute onion until soft. Add onion to meat and stir well. Add wine, tomatoes, water, parsley, dill, salt, and pepper. Cook at a low heat uncovered for 1/2 hour. Stir in cheese and bread crumbs, and cook 2 minutes longer. Remove from heat and let cool.

Cut, fill, and fold phyllo as in cheese triangle on page 22. Bake in a preheated 350° oven until golden brown, about 20 minutes. Makes 55 to 60 triangles.

Small Meatballs (Keftethakia)

I'm introducing this spiced, cocktail-sized meatball as an appetizer.

1 pound lean ground beef

3 slices white bread, crusts removed

1 egg, slightly beaten

1 onion, chopped fine

2 cloves garlic, minced

2 tablespoons chopped fresh mint or or 1 teaspoon dried mint

2 tablespoons chopped parsley

2 tablespoons red wine

1 teaspoon salt

1/2 teaspoon pepper

1/2 teaspoon cinnamon

1/2 cup flour

1/2 cup olive oil

2 tablespoons butter

1 cup beef broth or bouillon

Soak bread in water and squeeze dry. In a large bowl, combine meat, bread, egg, onion, garlic, mint, parsley, wine, salt, pepper, and cinnamon. Mix well with your hands until thoroughly blended. If mixture feels too firm, add small portion of water and mix well. Cover and chill in the refrigerator for 3 to 4 hours.

With floured hands form meat mixture into tiny balls. In a large frying pan, combine olive oil and butter and heat until a drop of water sizzles. Fry the meatballs, turning them to brown on all sides.

In a saucepan, bring the broth to a boil. Add meatballs and cook slowly for 10 minutes. Serve hot. Makes 45 tiny meatballs.

Stuffed Grape Leaves (Dolmathes Yalantzi)

Dolmathes (dol-MA-thez) are known in all of the Greek restaurants in the "Big Apple" as a medley of spices and rice wrapped in grape vine leaves, served with yogurt. Super!

1 jar vine leaves (about 3 dozen)

8 medium onions

3/4 cup olive oil

1 1/2 cups rice

1 cup parsley, finely chopped

1/4 cup fresh chopped dill

1/2 cup pine nuts

2 tablespoons dried mint

juice of 2 lemons

salt and pepper

Remove vine leaves from the jar, scald with hot water, and drain. Boil onions for 4 to 5 minutes. Drain, peel, and chop. In a skillet saute onions in a 1/2 cup of olive oil until soft. Stir in rice, parsley, dill, pine nuts, mint, and juice of 1 lemon. Salt and pepper to taste. Cook, stirring, for 2 to 3 minutes over low heat. Remove from heat and let cool.

Select 6 to 8 grape leaves and line the bottom of a saucepan. They will protect the stuffed grape leaves from burning.

Cut off thick stems from the remaining grape leaves. Place 1 teaspoon filling on underside of each leaf near stem end and fold base of leaf over filling. Then fold sides to enclose filling; roll lightly toward point. Layer stuffed grape leaves seam sides down on the grape leaves covering the bottom of the sauce pan.

Pour in remaining 1/4 cup olive oil and lemon juice. Weigh down with a heavy heatproof plate. Cover and simmer for 10 minutes over low heat. Pour in enough boiling water to cover stuffed grape leaves and simmer for 45 minutes longer.

Though often considered an appetizer, serve along with crusty bread and imported feta cheese for a full meal. Makes 45 to 50.

| 1) Place filling near stem of leaf. | 2) Fold base of leaf over filling. | 3) Fold one side over bottom. | 4) Fold second side; roll up leaf. |

Shrimp in Grape Leaves

Athenaeus incorporated the notion of harmony. The Greeks managed to get it into food as in everything else. There was a balance and measured interaction, like music. The notion of harmony fascinates me.

As Athenaeus put it almost 2,000 years ago, "The beginning and the root of everything good is the pleasure of the belly."

1   (8-ounce) jar vine leaves

$^1/_2$ pound sheep's milk feta cheese

2   tablespoons olive oil

2   tablespoons red wine vinegar

1   teaspoon dried marjoram

black pepper

1$^1/_4$ pound medium shrimp, shelled, and deveined

1   cup fish stock or clam juice
    (see page 39 for fish stock)

Remove 30 vine leaves from jar. Separate and rinse well. Place in a pot with water to cover. Bring to boil and simmer until tender. Set aside.

In a bowl, combine cheese, olive oil, vinegar, and marjoram. Season with pepper to taste. With a fork, mash mixture into a paste.

Spread out each vine leaf and place a shrimp in the center. Place a tablespoon of cheese mixture on top of shrimp and fold over the edges of the leaf, wrapping tightly.

Place wrapped shrimp in shallow pan close together, seam side down. Add fish stock to cover leaves. Place a plate over the bundles to keep the leaves from opening. Bake in preheated 350° oven for 20 minutes.

Place on platter and serve. Makes 30 appetizers.

NOTE: Peloponnese grape leaves are sold in specialty supermarkets. Any unused grape leaves left over from this recipe can be refrigerated, covered in brine.

Meat Stuffed Grape Leaves (Dolmathes Avgolemono)

The Greek Village, a family taverna on the upper east side without the upper east side prices, serves the little rolls wrapped in grape leaves in egg-lemon sauce. Delicious!

1   jar (16 ounces) grape leaves
1½ pounds ground beef or lamb
4   onions, thinly sliced
1   clove garlic, minced
3   tablespoons parsley, chopped
3   tablespoons dill, chopped
1   teaspoon dried mint
1   teaspoon salt
¼ teaspoon pepper

¾ cup water
¼ cup pine nuts (optional)
¾ cup rice
juice of 2 lemons
2   egg yolks
2   tablespoons flour
2   cups hot beef broth or bouillon

Rinse off brine by floating grape leaves in a basin of cold water. Immerse them in boiling water and let them boil for 5 minutes to soften.

Heat butter and saute meat until brown. Push meat to one side of the pan and add onions. Saute onions until soft. Add garlic, parsley, dill, mint, salt, pepper, and ¾ cup water. Simmer for ½ hour. Stir in rice and remove from heat.

Line the bottom of a large skillet with 6 leaves. This will protect the stuffed grape leaves from burning. Lay leaf stem side up. Snip off stem with kitchen shears. Place 1 teaspoon filling on underside of each leaf near stem end and fold base of leaf over filling. Then fold sides in to enclose filling; roll lightly toward point. (See diagram on page 26.) Layer stuffed grape leaves, seam sides down, on the grape leaves covering the bottom of the saucepan. Pour in enough hot water to cover them. Add juice of 1 lemon. Weigh down with a heavy heatproof plate. Cover and simmer for about 1 hour.

In a saucepan beat the egg yolks. Beat in flour little by little. Pour in hot broth drop by drop, stirring constantly. Cook and stir over low heat until sauce thickens. Don't overboil. Remove from heat.

Add the juice of 1 lemon. Pour over stuffed grape leaves and serve immediately. This recipe makes a first course or an excellent appetizer. Serves 8 as a first course.

Marinated Eggplant (Marinata Melitzanes)

The eggplant originated in India and has become the queen of vegetables in all Near Eastern cooking from Greece to Persia. There are more ways to cook this vegetable than any other in the Greek vegetable kingdom.

1 firm eggplant, 1 pound

1 cup cumin dressing (recipe below)

1 large tomato, peeled and diced

1 large onion, chopped fine

1/2 cup finely minced parsley

Peel eggplant and slice in 1/4-inch slices. Spread eggplant slices in a glass baking dish, sprinkling both sides with salt. Cover and allow to stand for 45 minutes. Pour off liquid; rinse eggplant well and pat dry. Put eggplant in a steamer and steam until just tender. Do not overcook.

Put steamed eggplant back in the glass baking dish and pour cumin dressing over it. Allow eggplant to cool to room temperature. Cover and refrigerate for 2 hours.

One hour before serving, add tomatoes and onion. Sprinkle parsley over entire dish.

Cumin Dressing:

1/2 cup red wine vinegar

1/2 teaspoon salt

1/2 teaspoon ground cumin

1 cup water

2 tablespoons canola oil

2 tablespoons fresh lemon juice

1 tablespoon dijon mustard

1 tablespoon sugar

Dissolve salt in the vinegar. Add all other ingredients and mix well. Refrigerate in a jar with a tight fitting lid. Mix well before using. Dish can be served as an appetizer, salad, or side dish. Yields 3 cups.

Marinated Shrimp Special (Marinata Gharithes)

No one makes this marinated appetizer any better than Emily Gyann. Keep this appetizer in mind for your next party.

3 pounds large shrimp, cooked, shelled, deveined

1 pint miracle whip

2 red onions, thinly sliced

1/3 cup of lemon juice (fresh)

1 1/2 tablespoons sugar

1 tablespoon dried dill weed

Combine all ingredients and mix well. Chill overnight before serving. Accompany with crackers. Makes 30.

Spinach Peta (Spanakopita)

It is wonderful fun to prepare both of these pie recipes. Even guests who dislike spinach will be amazed by the taste of this spinach pita.

Filling 1

2 pounds spinach, finely chopped

1 tablespoon salt

1 pound feta cheese, crumbled

1 small onion, chopped fine

4 eggs, slightly beaten

2 tablespoons olive oil

dash salt and pepper

15 sheets phyllo

$^1/_2$ pound butter, melted

Wash spinach, and chop very fine. Sprinkle with 1 tablespoon salt and allow to stand 15 minutes. Squeeze spinach to remove excess moisture. (This is a very important step in making a good filling.)

Place spinach in a bowl and combine with cheese, onion, eggs, olive oil, and salt and pepper to taste. Mix well.

Arrange 9 fila, which have been brushed with butter, in a greased 10 x 15 inch pan and cover with spinach filling. Cover with 6 fila, brushing each with melted butter. Chill until firm. Cut through top layers to mark pieces. Bake in a preheated 350° oven for 45 minutes. Serve hot or at room temperature. Serves 20.

Filling 2

4 (10-ounce) packages frozen chopped spinach

8 ounces cream cheese

1 pound feta cheese

$^1/_2$ cup grated romano cheese (optional)

1 small onion, chopped fine

3 tablespoons olive oil

1 teaspoon salt

$^1/_4$ teaspoon pepper

IMPORTANT NOTE: Allow spinach to stand at room temperature to defrost completely (do not soak in water). Squeeze very dry and combine with remaining ingredients.

Spinach Triangles (Spanakopetakia)

1 pound phyllo
2 pounds fresh spinach, finely chopped (or 10 ounces frozen spinach, thawed)
1 tablespoon salt
1 pound feta cheese, crumbled
1 medium onion, chopped fine

4 eggs, slightly beaten
2 tablespoons olive oil
1 teaspoon dill
salt and pepper
1 cup butter, melted, for brushing phyllo

The most important step: Wash spinach and chop very fine. Sprinkle with 1 tablespoon salt and allow to stand 20 minutes. Squeeze spinach to remove all the excess moisture.

In a bowl combine spinach, cheese, onions, eggs, olive oil, and dill. Salt and pepper to taste. Follow procedures as directed in cheese triangle recipe on page 22. Makes 55 to 60 triangles.

Spinach Pie (Spanakopita)

For several years, Helen and I have been trying to perfect the spinach pie recipe handed down to us by our parents. We came up with more of a domestic taste. Let us hear your comments.

$1/4$ cup olive oil
1 cup onions, chopped fine
3 packages (10-ounce) frozen spinach, thawed and squeezed very dry
3 eggs
$1/2$ pound feta cheese, crumbled
$1/2$ pound ricotta cheese

$1/4$ cup parsley, chopped
$3/4$ tablespoon dill
    or 2 tablespoons fresh dill
$1/8$ teaspoon pepper
16 sheets phyllo
$3/4$ cup butter, melted

In a skillet, add olive oil and onions. Saute till golden brown. Combine spinach with onions. Remove from heat. In a large bowl, beat eggs with rotary beater. With a wooden spoon, stir in cheese, parsley, dill, pepper, and spinach-onion mixture. Mix well.

Arrange 8 fila, which have been brushed with butter, in a 13 x 9 x 2 baking pan, and cover evenly with spinach filling. Cover all with 8 fila, brushing each with melted butter. Cut through top layers to mark pieces. Bake in preheated 350° oven for 35 minutes, or until top crust is puffy and golden brown, Serve hot or at room temperature. Serves 20.

NOTE: Keep unused pastry leaves covered with damp kitchen towel (or damp paper towel) to prevent drying out.

Bread Salad (Fattoush)

The following two recipes are Armenian, which is so similar to our Greek cuisine.

4 loaves pita bread

4 small red tomatoes

salt

1 cucumber

1 bunch scallions, white part sliced thin

1 cup whole Italian flat-leaf parsley leaves

1 tablespoon basil

1 tablespoon mint

1 bunch watercress, stems removed

$^1/_2$ to $^3/_4$ cup olive oil

juice of 1 lemon

$^1/_8$ teaspoon cayenne pepper or black pepper

Split the pitas in half and toast. Break toasted halves into small pieces and set aside. Chop tomatoes, transfer to a bowl, and sprinkle salt over them. Peel cucumber. Cut in half lengthwise, remove the seeds, and chop the flesh. Place in a separate bowl.
Prepare the scallions, parsley, basil, mint, and watercress. Set aside.
When ready to serve, spread the bread on a large serving plate. Spread the chopped tomatoes, their juice, and the chopped cucumber over the bread. Pour the olive oil in a thin stream over the vegetables. Add the lemon juice, cayenne or black pepper, and salt. Sprinkle the scallions and herbs all over. Toss and serve at the table. It will serve 3 as a main course luncheon. Makes 6 appetizer servings.

Nina Terzian's Hummus

1 can ($15^1/_2$ ounces) chick peas

2 large cloves garlic

1 teaspoon salt

$^1/_3$ cup fresh lemon juice

$^1/_3$ cup tahini (sesame seed paste)

olive oil

paprika

minced fresh parsley

Drain the chick peas and rinse them under cold water. In a food processor, chop the garlic. Add the chick peas, salt, lemon juice, and 2 tablespoons cold water. Process until very smooth, about 3 minutes. Add the tahini paste and process an additional 2 minutes.
Spread the hummus in a shallow serving bowl. Drizzle the top with olive oil, then sprinkle on paprika and parsley. Serve as a dip at room temperature with wedges of pita bread or slices of fresh bread. Yields $2^1/_2$ cups.

Greek Cheese Pie

9-inch unbaked pie shell
$3/4$ pound feta cheese, cut into small pieces
1 cup light cream
3 eggs
$1/2$ teaspoon dried thyme leaves
1 teaspoon cornstarch
dash pepper
1 small clove garlic, crushed
9 large pitted ripe olives
7 large pitted green olives
1 pimento, cut into strips

Preheat oven to 425°. Prick crust well with fork and place in freezer for 10 minutes. Remove from freezer and bake pie shell 10 minutes. Cool.

Blend cheese in electric blender with cream and eggs until smooth. Add thyme, corn-starch, and pepper. Blend. Stir in garlic. Empty cheese into pie shell. Bake 10 minutes. Arrange olives over top; bake 25 minutes longer or until filling is set. Decorate with pimento strips. Serve warm. Makes 8 servings.

NOTE: This pie may be made early in the day and reheated for serving.

Baked Meatballs in Tomato Sauce (Keftedakia me Saltsa)

$1^1/4$ pounds ground chuck
$1/2$ cup bread crumbs
1 egg
1 teaspoon mustard
1 tablespoon chopped parsley
$1/2$ cup grated onions
$1/8$ teaspoon oregano

1 teaspoon dried mint
$1/8$ teaspoon cinnamon
dash of allspice and cloves
$3/4$ cup tomato sauce
$1/4$ cup water
1 teaspoon minced garlic

Combine all ingredients except tomato sauce and water and shape into 1-inch balls. Put in a well greased baking pan in preheated 450° oven; bake for 20 to 25 minutes turning halfway through baking time. Drain on absorbent paper. In a saucepan simmer tomato sauce with water for 5 to 10 minutes. Add meatballs to sauce and marinate in the refrigerator overnight. Simmer in casserole dish for 15 minutes and serve hot. It's called an appetizer.

Grilled Eggplant and Feta Cheese

I saw this dish in a takeout joint in a very fashionable street in Manhattan.

1 medium eggplant
$1/2$ cup olive oil
$1/4$ pound imported feta cheese
juice of one lemon
1 tablespoon oregano
salt and pepper to taste

Slice eggplant the long way, about $1/4$ inch thick. Salt each slice and allow to drain in a colander for 30 minutes. Rinse with cold water and pat dry with paper towels. In a skillet add small portion of olive oil, and grill at a low heat so not to burn them. Allow to cool. Roll each up with a small portion of feta cheese and secure with a toothpick. Drizzle a dressing of olive oil, lemon juice, salt and pepper, and oregano over each. Serve at room temperature.

NOTE: Swiss Alpine cheese may be substituted for people who wish a lower sodium intake.

Shish Kebab
(Souvlakia Meze)

5−6 pound leg of lamb, boned, trimmed, and cut in 1-inch cubes
$1/4$ cup olive oil
1 teaspoon dried oregano
1 bay leaf, crushed
2 cloves garlic, minced
1 cup onions, chopped fine
$1/2$ cup chopped green peppers
$1/4$ cup port wine
juice of 2 lemons
$1/4$ cup white vinegar
salt and pepper to taste

In a large bowl combine all ingredients (except lamb) and marinate. Stir to blend. Add lamb cubes and cover bowl with cellophane wrap. Place in refrigerator overnight for best results. Preheat oven to 375°. Thread meat on 6-inch skewers. Baking time about 15 minutes, turning over several times until done. They can be served over a bed of rice. Serve a small Greek salad and a glass of Greek wine, and it becomes a meal.

"But what I have accomplished in this art of mine, no play-actor has ever accomplished at all. This art of mine was an empire of smoke. I was a sour sauce maker at the Court of Seleucus, and in the household of Agathocles of Sicily I was the first to introduce the royal-lentil soup."

Demetrius in the play *Areopagile*, quoted in the Deipnosophistae, 200 AD

"Green cheese, dry cheese, crushed cheese, grated cheese, sliced cheese, cream cheese."

Antiphanes in Cyclops

SOUPS

Bean Soup (Fasolada)

I stole this excellent soup recipe from James Gekas, my father, who featured this bean soup daily in our restaurant. I'm sure with some crusty bread and feta cheese you can make a meal of it. Actually, I'm quite sure of it, having done it more than once myself.

1/2 pound dried white beans	1 can (10 ounces) tomato sauce
8 cups water	1/2 cup olive oil
1/2 cup chopped celery	3 tablespoons chopped parsley
2 cloves garlic, sliced	1 teaspoon salt
2 cups onions, sliced thin	1/2 teaspoon pepper

Wash beans and soak overnight in enough cold water to cover beans. Rinse and drain. Transfer to a large pot and add 8 cups of water. Heat to boil. Lower heat, cover, and simmer for 1 hour or until tender. Add the remaining ingredients and cook covered for 1 1/2 hours. If the soup is too thick, add cold water and simmer for a few minutes longer. Makes 8 servings.

Tomato and Basil Soup

Try this fresh-tasting soup as a first course for dinner or with a sandwich at lunch.

1 large onion, thinly sliced	1 teaspoon sugar
1 tablespoon olive oil	1/2 teaspoon salt
2 cups chicken broth	1/4 teaspoon pepper
6 medium tomatoes, peeled and quartered	2 tablespoons snipped fresh basil or 2 teaspoons dried crushed
1 can (6 ounces) tomato paste	

Cook onion in oil in large saucepan until tender but not browned. Stir in chicken broth, tomatoes, tomato paste, sugar, salt, and pepper. Heat to a boil; cover, reduce heat, and simmer 20 minutes. Add basil and simmer 5 minutes longer. Cool slightly.

Place about half of the tomato mixture in a blender container or food processor bowl. Cover and blend or process until smooth. Repeat with remaining mixture. Serve warm. You may garnish each serving with yogurt, if desired. Makes 4 servings.

Psarosoupa a la Grecian Style

1 clove garlic, chopped	4 4-ounce lobster tails
1 medium onion, chopped	$^1/_2$ pound cleaned calamari
3 stalks celery, chopped	1 pound fresh cod
2 carrots, chopped	1$^1/_2$ quarts fish stock
2 ounces olive oil	2 ounces tomato paste
$^1/_2$ pound medium shrimp	salt and pepper to taste

Saute garlic, onion, celery, and carrots in a saute pan with olive oil until half done. Add shrimp, lobster, calamari, and cod and simmer for 5 minutes.

In a large pot bring fish stock to boil. Add tomato paste and salt and pepper to taste. Add all other ingredients to pot and boil for 10 minutes.

This soup is actually a main course. Makes 4 servings.

Fish Stock

You really don't need a recipe to make your fish stock. It's simple—pick up fresh fish bones, skin, heads, and tails from the fish counter at your grocery store. Just tell your fishmonger what you are preparing and he will take care of you.

Rinse the bones in fresh water and then place in a soup pot. Add 1 quart of water for each pound of bones. Add a few chopped carrots, yellow onions and celery ribs, and a bit of salt and pepper. Bring to a boil; cover, reduce heat, and simmer for 1 hour. Strain the stock and discard the solid material. Chill.

Summer is a great time to enjoy light soups that contain fewer calories and less fat than cold weather cousins.

The beauty of making homemade soup is that you can toss just about anything into the pot that you like.

For light soups choose lean, low fat, and fresh ingredients. For instance, to lighten up a meaty family favorite use lean beef with more muscle than fat such as round or rump. And you can never have too many vegetables in a soup. Choose those that are in season and at their peak of freshness.

Vegetable Soup (Hortosoupa)

Greek ingenuity prevails in their vegetable soups. A mosaic of colors and flavors develop naturally when vegetables currently in season are used along with other available ingredients.

2 quarts broth or stock

2 cloves garlic, sliced

$1/2$ cup onions, chopped

1 leek, chopped

1 large stalk celery, chopped

1 turnip, chopped

$1/4$ small head cabbage, shredded

1 medium potato, diced

2 tablespoons (dried peas, lentils, beans, soaked)

2 tablespoons cracked wheat

herbs of your choice (bay leaf, parsley, dill, fennel, basil or mint, to taste)

$1/2$ cup tomato juice

salt and freshly ground pepper

Soak the dried peas, lentils, or beans in advance according to the package directions.

In a soup pot, bring the broth or stock to a boil, then add the vegetables and cracked wheat. Simmer until tender, about 1 hour, adding the desired herbs, tomato juice, salt, and pepper after the first 30 minutes. Check for amount of liquid in the soup; it should be thick but may be thinned by adding more broth, stock, or water. Taste for seasoning and serve hot, sprinkled with additional herbs. Makes 2 quarts.

Lentil Soup #1 (Faki Soupa)

This is a great favorite of mine. I often make this soup at home.

1 pound lentils	2 beef boullion cubes
8¹/₂ cups water	1 tablespoon parsley
1 medium onion, chopped	1 teaspoon salt
1 tablespoon olive oil	pepper to taste
1 can (6 ounces) tomato paste	wine vinegar (optional)

Place lentils in a large pot and add water. Bring to a boil. Skim off foam. Simmer covered, 20 to 30 minutes, until lentils are tender. In a separate pan, saute onions in oil. Add onions to lentils. Mix in tomato paste, boullion, parsley, salt, and pepper. Bring to a boil. Cover and simmer 10 minutes longer. Serve with fresh parsley and a few dashes of vinegar sprinkled on top. Crusty bread is a must. Makes 8 servings.

Lentil Soup #2 (Faki Soupa)

This soup is very rich and tasty. It is also high in nutritional value. Faki is "soul food" for many Hellenes. One of the most ancient of dishes, its ancient name has survived along with its popularity. As cultural food, when made without oil, it is fare on the strictest fasting day: Good Friday.

1 pound lentils	¹/₂ cup olive oil
2 quarts water	1 tablespoon tomato paste
1 cup celery, chopped	1 bay leaf
1 medium onion, sliced thin	salt and pepper to taste
2 cloves garlic, chopped fine	2 tablespoons white vinegar (optional)

Wash lentils and soak in lukewarm water for 2 hours. Drain lentils and then add 2 quarts of water, celery, onions, and garlic. Bring to boil, cover, and simmer for ¹/₂ hour. Add olive oil, tomato paste, bay leaf, and salt and pepper. Simmer for 15 minutes or until lentils are tender. Makes 8 servings.

Yellow Split Pea Soup (Fava Soupa)

This has been a popular soup in Greece for many years, and has carried over to our country. It's a frugal dish, and also filling. A novice won't have any problems preparing this recipe.

1   pound yellow split peas
2   onions
$^1/_2$ cup olive oil
salt
juice of 1 lemon

Wash peas with cold water. In a pot, cook peas in enough cold water to cover peas. Bring to a boil. To boiling water add one quartered onion; reduce heat and simmer for 1 hour or until peas are soft.

Run peas through sieve, add salt to taste. Add 4 tablespoons olive oil and simmer for 5 minutes, stirring continuously. Serve in deep dinner plates and sprinkle with finely chopped onion, lemon juice, and remaining olive oil. Serve with crusty bread or pita bread. Makes 4 servings.

Chicken Rice Soup (Soupa Avgolemono)

Avgolemono soup has a traditional place in Greek culture, especially in the villages. Who knows how many families have survived mainly on soup over the centuries?

This soup must be considered one of the classic soups of the world. Avgolemono soup is made using chicken broth and rice with avgolemono, unless otherwise specified. Sometimes very fine vermicelli or orzo is substituted for rice.

6   cups chicken broth
$^1/_2$ cup long grain rice or $^3/_4$ cup orzo
3   eggs
juice of 1 large lemon
salt and pepper to taste

Bring broth to a full boil in a soup kettle. Gradually add the rice and salt, stirring constantly until the broth boils again. Reduce heat, cover, and simmer until the rice is tender, 12 to 14 minutes, taking care not to overcook. Remove from heat.

Separate eggs. Beat whites until peaks form. Add yolks and beat until blended. Add lemon, stirring until barely mixed. Gently stir two ladlefuls of soup into egg mixture. Pour this combined mixture back into soup, making certain soup does not boil or else curdling will result. Stir gently. Ladle into soup bowls.

Serve before a main course or with crusty bread, feta cheese, and a salad. Pass the peppermill at the table for additional zest. Makes 8 servings.

Celery Egg-Lemon Soup (Selino Avgolemono Soupa)

This recipe is a variation on the traditional avgolemono soup, only that the celery replaces the rice. Try it!

4 cups chicken broth

2 celery hearts, chopped

salt and pepper

2 eggs, separated

juice of 1 lemon

In a pot, combine broth with celery and season with salt and pepper to taste. Bring to a boil; cover, reduce heat, and simmer until celery is tender, but not overdone.

Prepare and add egg-lemon mixture according to the method described in chicken rice soup on the previous page. For a slight variation of flavor, add some finely chopped celery leaves. Serve hot with plenty of crusty bread for soaking. Makes 4 servings.

Lamb Shanks Soup (Soupa Botsari)

This is a great dish, and talk about frugal. Is this considered a soup? It's actually a good wholesome meal. Very Greek!

4 lamb shanks

8 cups water

1/4 cup butter

2 onions, chopped

1 head romaine lettuce, thinly sliced

1 bunch scallions, including parts of green top, chopped

1 cup rice, cooked

salt and pepper

2 eggs

juice of 1 lemon

1 tablespoon dried dill

1 bay leaf (optional)

Trim fat off shanks; place in a large pot and add water. Bring to boil. Skim off froth, cover, and simmer for 1 to 2 hours or until meat is tender. Strain the broth and set aside. Remove meat from shanks and cut into small bite-sized chunks; set aside.

In a large saucepan, melt butter and saute onions, scallions, and romaine. Add to broth and boil for 6 minutes. Add meat, rice, and salt and pepper to taste.

Beat eggs until frothy. Slowly add lemon juice, beating all the while. Add 1 cup of hot broth, drop by drop at the beginning and then increase the pouring, beating eggs constantly. Pour the sauce slowly into the soup and stir. Sprinkle with dill. Accompany with crusty bread and a glass of red wine. Makes 8 servings.

Spinach Soup (Spanaki Soupa)

This is a great favorite of mine, because I love spinach in any form. My adding chicken broth gives the spinach soup an extra dimension.

3   tablespoons unsalted butter
1   cup water
1   large onion, finely chopped
1   carrot, peeled and sliced
1   celery rib, sliced
6   cups chicken broth
6   large bunches fresh spinach, stems removed
salt and pepper to taste
parmesan cheese, grated
croutons

In a large kettle melt butter. Add water, onion, carrot, and celery. Cook until very soft. Add chicken broth and bring to a boil. Add spinach and cook uncovered 2 minutes until spinach wilts.
In a food processor, puree soup, a portion at a time, until very smooth. Transfer to large bowl. Add salt and pepper and serve immediately. Color of soup will change if soup is allowed to stand. Garnish with grated cheese and croutons, if desired. Makes 10 servings.

Lentil and Brown Rice Soup

This soup is very nutritious. It is high in carbohydrates, protein, and fiber, yet very low in fat.

6   cups low-sodium chicken broth
2   cups water
1$^{1}/_{2}$ cups lentils, picked over and rinsed
1   cup brown rice
1   can (28 ounces) whole tomatoes, broken up and undrained
3   carrots, peeled, halved lengthwise, and cut into $^{1}/_{4}$ inch slices
1   cup chopped onions
$^{1}/_{2}$ cup chopped celery
3   cloves garlic, minced
$^{1}/_{2}$ teaspoon each, dried and crushed: basil, oregano, thyme
1   bay leaf
$^{1}/_{2}$ cup fresh parsley, minced
2   tablespoons red wine vinegar
black pepper to taste

Mix chicken broth, water, lentils, rice, undrained tomatoes, carrots, onions, celery, garlic, basil, oregano, thyme, and bay leaf in a large dutch oven. Heat soup to a boil; reduce heat, cover, and simmer until lentils and rice are tender (55 minutes), stirring occasionally.
Remove and discard bay leaf. Stir in parsley, vinegar, and pepper. If necessary, thin the soup with additional water or broth. Makes 10 servings.

Tripe Soup

1 pound tripe, cut into 1-inch strips	8 ounces water
1 lamb head	2 egg yolks
1 teaspoon salt	1 tablespoon cornstarch
1/2 teaspoon white pepper	2 ounces lemon juice
1 teaspoon garlic powder	

Cut tripe open with a sharp knife and clean the inside thoroughly under running water. Fill a soup pot with water and add tripe and lamb head; cook for 1 1/2 hours. Remove lamb head from pot and strain, saving all juices. Use a fork to remove all meat from lamb head and cut into small pieces. In the pot with the juices from the lamb head, combine your tripe and lamb head meat. Add salt, pepper, garlic powder, and water. Boil for 30 minutes. Remove from heat and let cool for 15 minutes.

In a bowl, beat egg yolks well. Add cornstarch and lemon juice to yolks, beating until cornstarch is dissolved. Add the juices from the lamb head and tripe to egg mixture, and mix well. Pour mixture into pot with lamb meat and tripe. Mix well and serve hot. Makes 4 servings.

Fish Soup With Egg and Lemon Sauce
(Psarosoupa me Avgolemono)

Just as the "Bird Nest" soup originated in China—fish stew was invented by the Greeks. You can also say that avgolemono sauce is a Greek classic. Combine the two and we have a rich fish soup with egg and lemon flavor.

3   pounds white fish

1   tablespoon salt

juice of 1 lemon

8   cups water

1   medium onion, sliced

1   carrot, sliced

1   stalk celery with leaves

$^1/_2$ cup olive oil

1   bay leaf (optional)

4 to 5 peppercorns

$^1/_2$ cup rice

egg and lemon sauce (see page 64)

parsley

lemon and olive oil

salad dressing or mayonnaise

Clean and wash fish. The fish can be cut into large pieces or left whole. Rub with 1 teaspoon salt and lemon juice.

Put into a large saucepan the water, vegetables, remaining salt, oil, bay leaf, and peppercorns. Cook over a medium heat for 35 minutes. Reduce the heat to simmering point. Add the fish and cook slowly for 16 to 18 minutes.

Remove the fish from pot and keep it hot on the side. Strain the stock and vegetables through a sieve and return to the pot. Add the rice and cook for 18 minutes.

Stir the egg and lemon sauce gradually into the soup and heat. Do not allow to boil or soup will curdle.

Serve fish soup in soup plates and sprinkle with chopped parsley. Serve the fish separately with latholemono (oil and lemon dressing) or cover with mayonnaise. Makes 6 to 8 servings.

Greek Easter Soup (Mageritsa)

It is traditional for the Greek family to go to church for midnight services on Easter eve, and then return home and end the long lenten fasting by enjoying the Mageritsa, which is eaten only at Easter time.

1 honeycomb tripe

1 pound lamb or calf liver

4 cans (13³/₄ ounces each) beef broth

1 bunch dill weed, finely chopped

1 bunch scallions, including 4 inches
  of green tops, finely chopped

2¹/₂ teaspoons salt

¹/₄ teaspoon pepper

2 cups long grain rice

6 eggs

1 cup fresh lemon juice

Boil tripe and liver in 3¹/₂ quarts of water, skimming foam when needed. Reduce heat, cover, and simmer for 2 to 3 hours. Remove from heat.

Remove meat from stock, saving stock. Cut meat into very small pieces and set aside. Strain stock through a cheesecloth into a large pot. Add beef broth and bring to a boil. Add diced meat, dill, scallions, salt, and pepper; simmer for 15 minutes. This may all be done ahead of time and refrigerated.

One hour before serving, add rice to soup. Simmer until tender, about 20 minutes. Remove soup from heat. To prepare avgolemono, separate eggs and beat whites until peaks form. Add yolks and beat until blended well. Slowly add lemon juice, stirring all the while. Gently stir 3 ladlefuls of broth into avgolemono. Pour the mixture back into the soup pot, stirring gently. Serve immediately. This soup also freezes well. Makes 10 servings.

SALADS

Santorini's Tomato Salad (Domatasalata)

I believe the restaurants in Astoria must be importing tomatoes from the Santorini Island, where they claim to have a rich volcanic soil which produces the sweetest tomatoes in all of Greece.

8   medium ripe tomatoes

5   scallions, chopped

1   cucumber, peeled and thinly sliced

1   teaspoon oregano

$^1/_4$ cup olive oil

salt and pepper to taste

Cut tomatoes into small pieces directly into a large bowl. Add remaining ingredients and toss lightly. Let stand for several minutes before serving. This salad tastes best at room temperature. Crumbled feta cheese goes well as a topping. Accompany with French bread for soaking. Makes 6 servings.

Lettuce Salad (Maroulosalata)

In Greece, salads may be served as appetizers, as a first course, on a separate plate with the fish or meat course, as a garnish, or simply brought to the table in a large bowl to be passed around to the entire party. Marouli (lettuce) is also preferred cooked with meat, with or without avgolemono.

Discard the outer leaves of the lettuce. Wash and cut into very thin strips with a sharp knife. Add sliced onions and chopped fresh dill. Sprinkle with salt, olive oil, lemon juice, or vinegar dressing.

Tomato and Cucumber Salad (Angourotomatosalata)

This salad is a favorite among American tourists at the Taverna Sigalad in Athens, located in Monastiraki Square.

1   pound tomatoes, sliced

1   cucumber, peeled and sliced

1   onion, sliced thin

olive oil and lemon juice or vinegar dressing

dried oregano or chopped parsley

Cucumbers and tomatoes were brought in from Asia centuries ago. Combine these garden delights together well. A great treat especially on hot days. Makes 4 servings.

Asparagus with Lemon Oil Dressing (Asparagos Latholemono)

2 pounds asparagus

salt

1 sprig fresh basil, marjoram, or rosemary

$^1/_2$ cup olive oil and lemon or vinegar salad dressing
(see page 62)

capers for garnish

Trim the asparagus spears with a small sharp knife to remove the tough outer parts of the stalk. Cut off and discard the tough butt ends, wash thoroughly, and drain. In an enameled pan with a removable rack, fill with water to a level of 3 inches and lightly season with salt and herb. Bring to a boil and place the asparagus in the rack with tips up. Partially cover the pan and cook until tender but firm, not limp and mushy (8 to 12 minutes depending on the diameter). Lift the rack and arrange the asparagus (without breaking) on a warm platter. Pour dressing over asparagus. Makes 6 to 8 servings.

Boiled Wild Greens (Vrasta Agria Horta)

My aunts and cousins living in upstate New York would commonly take Sunday drives in the country, looking for patches of tender mustard greens (sinapia) or dandelions (radikia). The key is to find ones at the right moment, before they flower and become too bitter to cook.

The tender plants are dug up, sometimes roots and all, and taken home to be washed in cold water until they are thoroughly cleaned.

1 pound greens

$^1/_4$ cup olive oil

juice of 1 lemon

Place greens in boiling salt water and cook till soft and tender. Drain greens, Pour olive oil and squeeze lemon juice over greens. Mix well.

Goes well with broiled fish, lamb chops, or pork chops. Makes 4 servings.

Cucumber Salad with Yogurt (Tsatziki)

A refreshing salad sure to please during the summer time. Experience it!

2 or 3 cucumbers, peeled and thinly sliced
1 teaspoon white vinegar
1 teaspoon spearmint flakes
1 teaspoon scallions, finely chopped
$^1/_2$ teaspoon sugar
salt and pepper
1 cup yogurt

In a small bowl, mix cucumbers with vinegar, spearmint flakes, scallions, sugar, and salt and pepper to taste. Add yogurt and stir gently to combine. Cover and chill 2 hours or more. Serve salad style on lettuce leaves and garnish with tomato wedges, or as a dip with crusty bread. Makes 4 servings.

Fresh Broccoli Salad (Brokola Salata)

Though former president George Bush has expressed not liking this wonderful green vegetable, I love it in any shape or form. Sorry, George!

3 to 4 pounds fresh broccoli
salt
$^1/_2$ cup olive oil
juice of 2 lemons

Wash the broccoli and trim. Place heads upwards in boiling salted water in a saucepan. Cover and cook for about 20 minutes, or until tender; drain immediately. Beat olive oil and lemon juice, and spoon over broccoli. Makes 4 servings.

Grecian Boiled Endive (Vrasta Antidia)

This vegetable is a Greek favorite, not only in restaurants, but also served at homes. Endive was one of the earliest vegetables that Greeks cultivated. Found growing wild in the fields, Greeks soon had their own garden plots of this tender, leafy, green vegetable.

2 heads of endive

¼ teaspoon salt

cruet of olive oil

fresh lemon juice

Cut off roots of endive and rinse endive 2 to 3 times with cold water. Place in large pot. Sprinkle with salt. Cover and steam for 30 minutes or until tender. Serve with olive oil and lemon juice. This traditional vegetable will complement any broiled meat or fish. Don't forget some imported feta, and crusty bread for soaking. Makes 4 servings.

Fresh Spinach Salad (Spanaki Salata)

Salata, for most Greeks, means one seasonal vegetable, served raw or cooked, hot or cold, seasoned with olive oil and lemon or vinegar. Greek people in America alternate their local favorites between spinach, horta, squash, and beets. This spinach salad is a delight!

1 pound fresh spinach

½ cup crumbled feta

¾ cup olive oil

juice of 1 lemon

½ teaspoon salt

pepper to taste

Wash spinach several times in cold water. Drain thoroughly and place spinach in a medium-size bowl. Sprinkle with feta cheese. Combine remaining ingredients and beat until creamy. Drizzle over spinach, and toss lightly to mix ingredients. For a complete meal, quarter two hard-boiled eggs, twelve calamata olives, and a loaf of crusty bread. Makes 2 to 3 servings.

Artichoke and Crab Meat Salad (Aginara Kavoura)

Yes—New York restaurants enjoy creating salads, especially during lunch hours. Whether it's winter or summer time, you'll love this salad.

8 medium artichokes
1 cup crab meat
1/4 cup chopped ripe olives
3/4 cup olive oil
2 or 3 lemons
salt and pepper

Remove the tough outer leaves of artichokes. Cut off part of stems one inch from the tips. Cut artichokes in half lengthwise and scoop out the choke. Drop rest of artichoke into boiling, salted water seasoned with the juice of 1 lemon and 1 tablespoon olive oil. Simmer for 30 minutes or until tender. Drain well and put into a salad bowl. Add crab meat and chopped olives. Whip oil and lemon juice. Add salt and pepper to taste. Mix all ingredients well. Makes 4 to 6 servings.

Greek Salad (Salata a la Greque)

Salads accompany every Greek dinner and range from classic lettuce to combinations like spinach and feta, cucumber and yogurt, green beans and tomatoes, or onion and feta. Best known is the Greek Salad—a meal in itself. Always use olive oil and fresh lemon juice or wine vinegar.

small head iceberg lettuce
small cucumber, sliced
small green pepper, sliced thin
1 tomato, in wedges
2 scallions, thinly sliced
12 calamata olives
6 salonika peppers

1/2 cup feta cheese, crumbled
anchovy fillets
1 teaspoon oregano
salt and pepper
olive oil
wine vinegar

In a large wooden salad bowl, tear lettuce into bite size pieces. Toss with cucumber, green pepper, tomato, and scallions. Garnish with olives, peppers, feta cheese, and anchovies. Sprinkle with oregano, and salt and pepper to taste. Mix well and drizzle olive oil and vinegar in equal amounts over salad. Toss lightly. Makes for a super lunch. Serve with crusty bread and white wine. Makes 3 to 4 servings.

Aegean Salad (Lima Beans, Cucumbers, and Radishes)
(Aegean Salata)

1 cup dried baby lima beans

1 cup peeled, diced cucumber

$^1/_2$ cup sliced and quartered radishes

$1^1/_2$ tablespoons chopped fresh dill

15 calamata olives

1 red onion, sliced thin

$^1/_4$ cup of virgin olive oil

1 tablespoon red wine vinegar

1 teaspoon oregano

salt to taste

Soak lima beans overnight. Simmer fresh limas in water until cooked but still firm. Drain and place in cold water to stop cooking. In a serving bowl combine lima beans, cucumber, radishes, dill, olives, and onions. In a small jar combine olive oil, vinegar, oregano, and salt. Shake well. Pour over salad and toss lightly. Serves 4 as a side dish.

EGGS &
OMELETTES

Zucchini Omelette (Kolokithakea me Avga)

The basic rules for a good omelette: use an aluminum pan with sloping sides. The pan should have a metal handle so that it can be put under a broiler if you wish. Use the pan for omelettes only, and once you have cured it, don't wash it with soap—ever. Wash with hot water only.

Fill the center of your omelettes with zucchini and other wonderful vegetables.

1/4 cup olive oil

2 cups zucchini, cubed

2 tablespoons onion, chopped fine

dash of oregano

salt and pepper

5 eggs, beaten

Heat oil until hot; fry zucchini and onions until zucchini is tender and onions are soft. Season with a dash of oregano and salt and pepper to taste. Pour the beaten eggs over zucchini, lifting the edges of zucchini cubes so the eggs run evenly over them. Cook slowly, running a spatula around the edge and lifting egg mixture to allow uncooked portion to flow underneath. Cook until eggs are firm, and slide onto a serving platter. Serve a plate of tomato wedges and slices of feta cheese. Makes 2 to 3 servings.

Tomato Omelette (Avga me Domates)

2 fresh tomatoes, peeled and chopped

3 tablespoons olive oil

2 tablespoons butter

pinch of oregano

salt and pepper

1 tablespoon water

6 eggs, beaten

Heat olive oil in a skillet. Saute the tomatoes very gently and simmer for 5 to 7 minutes. Season with salt and pepper to taste, and a pinch of oregano. Add butter. Beat eggs with 1 tablespoon of water. Fold beaten eggs into tomato mixture in skillet. Allow the eggs to cook slightly, then fold eggs over the tomatoes with a spatula, and cook a few minutes longer. Serve hot. Accompany by crusty bread and feta cheese. Makes 2 to 3 servings.

Oven Omelette with Ground Beef (Sfougato)

The island of Rhodes is the author of this tasty creation. Experience it!

$^1/_2$ cup butter

3   medium onions, chopped

1   pound lean ground beef

2   pounds zucchini, cubed

2   teaspoons salt

$^1/_2$ teaspoon pepper

1   teaspoon dill

1   tablespoon parsley

1   cup hot water

4   eggs, beaten

bread crumbs

Melt butter in a deep frying pan. Add onions; cook until onions are tender but not browned. Add meat and saute for 10 minutes. Add zucchini, salt, pepper, dill, parsley, and 1 cup hot water. Cover and simmer for $^1/_2$ hour, stirring occasionally. Let cool.
Beat eggs slightly and add to the meat mixture. Grease a 2-quart baking dish and sprinkle with bread crumbs. Pour the mixture into baking dish and bake at 325° for 25 minutes or until firm. Makes 5 to 6 servings.

Feta Cheese Omelette (Avga me Feta)

3   tablespoons butter, melted

4   eggs, beaten

$^1/_4$ cup feta cheese, crumbled

oregano, pinch

olive oil, dash

Melt butter in a skillet; lower heat and add beaten eggs, shaking the pan to spread eggs evenly and to keep them from sticking. Cook eggs slowly, running a spatula around the edge and lifting egg mixture to allow uncooked portion to flow underneath.
When the eggs are almost cooked, place feta cheese in the center, and sprinkle with oregano and dash of olive oil. Fold the omelette over the cheese on both sides, and cook a few minutes longer. Slide onto serving platter. Serve with fresh tomato wedges and crusty bread. Makes 2 servings.

Greek Omelette for Two (Omeletta)

I know that when you think of Greek cooking, omelettes don't even enter your mind—but after reading this egg omelette recipe, you may alter your thinking.

This can be made with ingredients that you probably have on hand. So if you're having unexpected guests, this is a good problem-solver.

$^1/_2$ of a 10-ounce package frozen chopped spinach

$^1/_4$ cup crumbled feta cheese (1 ounce)

$^1/_4$ cup cream-style cottage cheese

2 teaspoons minced dried onion

$^1/_4$ teaspoon dried mint leaves, crushed

dash of pepper

3 or 4 eggs

1 tablespoon butter

In a medium saucepan, cook spinach according to package directions; drain well. In same pan, combine spinach, cheeses, onion, mint, and pepper. Heat thoroughly over low heat, stirring occasionally. Meanwhile, beat eggs; season with salt and pepper. Melt butter in an 8- or 10-inch skillet. (For a 3-egg omelette, use 8-inch skillet, for a 4-egg omelette, 10-inch pan.) Add eggs; cook slowly, running a spatula around the edge and lifting egg mixture to allow uncooked portion to flow underneath. Spoon spinach mixture onto one-half of omelette; fold other side over filling. Slide onto serving platter. Makes 2 servings.

SAUCE AND
TOPPINGS

Yogurt Salad Dressing (Yiaourti Mayonnaisa)

This dressing is tart and tangy. It's excellent over lettuce and other greens.

1 cup yogurt	1/2 teaspoon oregano
1 clove garlic, minced	1/2 teaspoon salt
1 teaspoon vinegar	1/2 teaspoon sugar
2 ounces blue cheese	pinch of pepper
1/2 teaspoon dry mustard	

Blend ingredients together. Keep refrigerated for 2 hours. You can love this tasty dressing over a large family-size salad, or spooned over crusty or pita bread...the possibilities are endless. Yields 1 cup.

Bechamel Sauce (Saltsa Besmel)

I know this white sauce has a French name, but it actually was invented by the Greeks. This white sauce was served in Greece over 125 years before it was ever introduced in France.

4 tablespoons butter	dash of nutmeg (optional)
6 tablespoons flour	2 cups milk
1 teaspoon salt	2 eggs (optional)
1/4 teaspoon pepper	

In a small saucepan, melt butter over low heat. Add flour, salt, pepper, and nutmeg; stir until well blended. Remove from heat. Gradually stir in milk and return to heat. Cook, stirring constantly, until thick and smooth. With eggs: When sauce is thick, remove from heat and gradually add 2 slightly beaten eggs, stirring constantly. Yields 3 cups.

Olive Oil and Lemon or Vinegar Salad Dressing

1/3 cup olive oil	salt and pepper
2 to 3 tablespoons lemon juice or vinegar	generous pinch of oregano

In a small bowl combine olive oil and lemon juice or vinegar. Add salt, pepper, and oregano; mix well.

Olive oil and lemon salad dressing is served with boiled or grilled fish, and with any cooked or raw vegetable salad. Olive oil and vinegar salad dressing is served with uncooked salads. Yields 1/2 cup.

Tomato Sauce (Saltsa Domata)

2 pounds tomatoes or
   or 1 can (20 ounces) tomatoes

1/2 cup onions, chopped fine

1 clove garlic, chopped fine

3 tablespoons butter

1/8 teaspoon sweet basil

1/8 teaspoon thyme

1 bay leaf

2 tablespoons chopped parsley

1 teaspoon flour (optional)

salt, pepper, and sugar to taste

If using fresh tomatoes, scald, peel, and chop tomatoes coarsely. In a saucepan, saute onions and garlic in butter until golden brown. Add tomatoes, herbs, and seasonings and bring to a boil. Lower flame and simmer gently until thoroughly cooked (30 to 40 minutes). To thicken the sauce, mix teaspoon of flour with cold water, add to sauce, and cook a few minutes longer. You'll love this sauce over meatballs, spaghetti, or noodles. Yields 3 cups.

Sauce Vinaigrette (Saltsa Vinegarette)

1/2 cup olive oil

1/4 cup vinegar

2 tablespoons lemon juice

1 hard-boiled egg, chopped

1 teaspoon chopped capers

2 teaspoons minced sweet pickle

2 teaspoons chopped parsley

1 teaspoon onion, chopped fine

Beat oil, vinegar, and lemon juice together. Add the remaining ingredients. Mix well. Serve over boiled fish, boiled meats, or shell fish. Yields 2 cups.

Lemon Mayonnaise (Lemoni me Mayonnaisa)

1/3 cup mayonnaise

1 tablespoon cream

1 teaspoon lemon juice

In a small bowl, combine mayonnaise, cream, and lemon juice. Stir until blended. Refrigerate. Serve over salads, fish, and vegetables. Yields 1/3 cup.

Mayonnaise (Mayonnaisa)

3 egg yolks, large eggs

1 teaspoon salt

dash cayenne or white pepper

1 cup olive oil

2 tablespoons lemon juice

In a small bowl, beat egg yolks at medium speed with a mixer. Add salt and cayenne; beat until thick and lemon colored. Add ¼ cup oil, one drop at a time, beating until thick. Gradually add 1 tablespoon lemon juice, beating after each addition. Add ½ cup oil in a steady slow stream, beating constantly. Slowly add remaining lemon juice and follow with remaining oil, beating constantly. Cover and refrigerate until ready to use. Yields 1¼ cups.

Egg and Lemon Sauce (Saltsa Avgolemono)

This is the basic sauce in Greek cooking. It is used many ways in many recipes. Always use fresh lemon juice. Whenever possible, use the stock in which the dish was cooked. If fresh stock is not available, use canned broth or diluted chicken stock base.

3 eggs

juice of 2 lemons

1 cup hot broth, preferably from the dish the sauce accompanies

salt and pepper

Beat eggs until frothy. Add lemon juice slowly, beating constantly. Add 1 tablespoon of hot broth to beaten eggs and stir. Slowly add remaining broth, stirring constantly with a spoon (this keeps eggs from curdling). Pour hot sauce over food and serve immediately. Salt and pepper to taste. Yields 2 cups.

Hollandaise Sauce (Saltsa Ollandiki)

We Greeks admit that the French invented this rich lemon sauce and for this we love the French.

4 cold egg yolks

juice of 1 lemon

12 tablespoons cold butter

salt

cayenne pepper

In a small saucepan, combine egg yolks and lemon juice. Place over low heat and add butter, 1 tablespoon at a time. Stir constantly with a wire whisk until sauce thickens, 3 to 5 minutes. When desired consistency is reached, remove from heat. Add salt and cayenne to taste. Serve on vegetables, poached eggs, and meats. Yields 2 cups.

Tomato Sauce with Olive Oil (Saltsa Domata me Lathi)

The Greeks enjoy good sauces. They are generally cooked into the dish, rather than put on top.

This is a basic sauce used in Greek kitchens. Make yourself a batch, and refrigerate for future cooking.

Use this wonderful sauce with fish, meats, vegetables, and rice dishes.

1/2 cup olive oil	1 1/2 teaspoons salt
2 cloves garlic, chopped	1/4 teaspoon pepper
chopped parsley	1 tablespoon sugar
2 pounds fresh ripe tomatoes, peeled and sliced	1/4 teaspoon dried basil

Heat oil in saucepan. Add garlic and 3 tablespoons parsley, and cook slowly for 3 minutes. Add remaining ingredients, cover, and cook over a very low heat for 45 minutes or until thick. Yields 2 cups.

Sun Dried Tomato Sauce

3 ounces sun dried tomatoes	1 12-ounce can Italian plum tomatoes
4 ounces marsala wine, sweet	1/4 cup fresh basil, cut into thin strips
1/2 cup onions, chopped fine	2 bay leaves
1/4 cup carrots, chopped small	black pepper to taste
3 cloves garlic, chopped fine	1/2 teaspoon red pepper flakes
3 ounces olive oil	2 tablespoons parsley, chopped

Soak sun dried tomatoes in warm wine until soft. Puree tomato-wine mixture. Saute vegetables in olive oil until soft; add garlic and saute 30 seconds longer. Chop plum tomatoes; add to vegetables along with sun dried tomatoes and wine. Cook over low heat for 20 minutes. Add herbs and cook another 20 minutes. Put in food processor and pulse on and off for 5 to 10 seconds. Serve warm. Yields 2 cups.

Yogurt (Yiaourti)

Very simple—Make your own!

1 quart milk	3 tablespoons yogurt
1/2 cup cream	

Bring milk and cream to boil over a low heat, stirring constantly to prevent sticking. Simmer for 8 minutes. Remove from fire and leave to cool. In a cup pour a little milk and add yogurt, and dilute. Pour rest of milk and blend well. Take 2 small jars and fill with yogurt, covering both jars. Leave in a warm area overnight; when yogurt is set, place in your refrigerator. Makes one quart.

Garlic Sauce (Skordalia)

Skordalia is a mainstay of Greek cookery. My mother, bless her soul, fed us this wskordalia at least once a week, hoping that this strong garlic sauce would prevent us from getting colds during the cold winters. It worked!

1 head garlic (up to 8 cloves)	$^1/_3$ cup vinegar
1$^3/_4$ pounds potatoes, boiled and peeled	salt and pepper to taste
1 cup olive oil	

Clean garlic and mash completely. Mash in potatoes, one at a time, until you have a smooth, thick paste. Alternately add oil and vinegar, beating constantly, until oil is completely absorbed. Continue to beat until the sauce is stiff enough to hold its shape. Serve with fish, fried eggplant, or zucchini. Garlic lovers enjoy it mounted on crusty bread. Opaa!

Greek Tomato Sauce

A large percent of Greek restaurants in the "Big Apple" certainly point to the Middle Eastern and Turkish influence when adding allspice and cinnamon to this tasty sauce. Make yourself a big batch and refrigerate for your next dish of pasta or various cooked vegetables.

4 tablespoons olive oil	2 teaspoons oregano
1 medium yellow onion, peeled and chopped	1 cup red wine
	1 8-ounce can tomato sauce
6 ripe tomatoes, cored and coarsely chopped	$^1/_4$ teaspoon cinnamon
1 clove garlic, chopped fine	$^1/_8$ teaspoon allspice
2 tablespoons chopped parsley	salt and pepper to taste

Heat olive oil in a large skillet. Add onions and garlic; saute until clear. Add tomatoes, parsley, and oregano. Simmer, covered, until the tomatoes are tender, about 30 minutes. Add remaining ingredients and cook an additional 25 minutes.

NOTE: The sauce will keep well for several days in refrigerator.

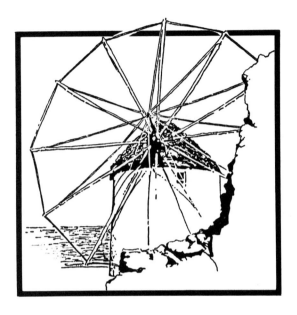

FISH AND
SEAFOOD

Broiled Whitefish with Lemon Herb Sauce

The symbol of the fish appears constantly in Greek art. Greeks drew simple fish designs on dishes and pots long before the Gnostics, an early sect of Christians, took it as a secret symbol for their faith.

The Greeks have evolved many ways to cook and serve fish and seafood. Some of the most common fish used are: carp, cod, red mullet, sea bass, halibut, smelts, swordfish, trout, and rockfish.

This dish is easy and quick to prepare and tastes fantastic.

2   pounds fresh whitefish fillets

$^1/_2$ cup butter

juice of 2 lemons

1 tablespoon oregano or thyme

salt and pepper to taste

Preheat broiler. Arrange fish fillets in "broil and serve" dish. Melt butter in small saucepan. Brush fish with one tablespoon of melted butter. Season with salt and pepper to taste. Broil for 14 minutes, or until brown and flaky. Remove fish from heat; add remaining ingredients to melted butter. Blend well and heat slowly. Pour over broiled fish. Serve with rice pilaf and a hot vegetable. Don't forget extra lemon wedges. Enjoy! Makes 4 to 6 servings.

Red Snapper a la Greek Style

Both ancient and modern Greeks have been devoted to the sea. Some of the favorite fish of the Greeks are, unfortunately, not available in this country. However, we do have in America an abundance of fish to keep alive the recipes and tradition of Greek fish cookery.

4   (1-pound) whole red snapper

olive oil

3   teaspoons salt

2   teaspoons oregano

$^1/_2$ teaspoon black pepper

4   cloves garlic, finely chopped

Lemon oil sauce:

1   cup olive oil

$^1/_2$ cup lemon juice

$^1/_4$ cup parsley, chopped

$^1/_2$ teaspoon salt

Wash fish, drain, and pat dry. Brush olive oil on all parts of fish. Set aside. In a bowl mix all the spices including garlic. Sprinkle spices all over fish and cavity. Let it stand for 30 minutes before broiling. Broil (or charco-broil) for 20 minutes or until brown and flaky.

For lemon oil sauce, mix all ingredients thoroughly in a saucepan and heat slowly. Spoon sauce over broiled fish. Serve with rice pilaf and a glass of dry white wine. Makes 4 servings.

Greek Style Broiled Snapper (Psari Tis Skaras)

No place in Greece is very far from the sea. Fish is therefore plentiful and extremely popular with many varieties to select from!

The Greeks are somewhat like the Chinese, who insist on fresh fish, and I mean alive, whenever possible.

The people of Greece have always enjoyed fish from the beginning of recorded history. There is good evidence to prove that the Greeks actually taught the Romans how to catch and appreciate fish.

^{1}/$_2$ cup olive oil

4 tablespoons margarine, melted

1 clove garlic, crushed

2 tablespoons grated parmesan cheese

1 teaspoon oregano

salt and pepper

4 tablespoons fresh lemon juice

1^1/$_2$ pounds red snapper fillets

In a bowl, combine olive oil, margarine, garlic, parmesan cheese, oregano, and salt and pepper to taste. Add lemon juice. Add fillets, turning to coat evenly. Cover bowl with plastic wrap and refrigerate 1 to 2 hours.

Drain fillets, reserving marinade. Cook fillets skin side down in a preheated broiler 12 to 13 minutes or until fish flakes easily when tested with fork. Brush fillets with marinade during broiling. Serve with rice pilaf and dry white Retsina wine. Makes 3 to 4 servings.

Fried Fish with Piquant Sauce (Psari Marianto)

This old recipe varies from household to household, though its essentials remain the same. A loveable dish because it can be served as an appetizer or a main course. Crusty bread is a must.

3¼ pounds whitefish, finger sized pieces
juice of 1 lemon
⅔ cup olive oil
3 tablespoons wine vinegar
½ cup dry white wine
1 10-ounce can tomatoes, sieved
3 sprigs rosemary
2 bay leaves

1 teaspoon dill
3 cloves garlic, chopped
2 teaspoons sugar
1 tablespoon parsley, chopped
¼ cup raisins
salt and pepper
flour

Clean and wash fish, sprinkle with lemon juice and dip in flour. Season to taste with salt and pepper.

Heat oil in a large frying pan and fry fish until golden brown, about 10 minutes. Set aside fish. Strain oil into a small bowl and clean frying pan. Pour back ⅓ cup of the strained oil and heat over a low heat. Add two tablespoons of flour, stirring until it begins to turn yellow. Stir in tomatoes, garlic, and all other ingredients, except the fish and remaining oil. Let sauce simmer over a very low heat for 10 minutes, stirring occasionally. Lay fish close together in a shallow bowl and cover fish with the sauce. Makes 6 servings.

Grilled Salmon with Dill Sauce (Psari Tighanitos)

So simple, and so delicious. Make sure you don't overcook. It cooks very fast, so be careful.

4 10-ounce fillets of salmon
oil for grilling

Dill sauce:

1 small onion, chopped
3 ounces butter
2 bay leaves
¼ cup fresh dill, chopped

pinch white pepper
½ teaspoon salt
½ pint heavy cream

In a skillet heat oil, and grill salmon for about 10 minutes.

In a saucepan, saute onions in butter until soft. Add bay leaves, fresh dill, salt, and pepper. Cook for 2 minutes. Add heavy cream and bring to a boil. Spoon sauce over grilled fish. Great served with green beans, tomatoes, and feta cheese. A dry white wine also goes well. Makes 4 servings.

Grilled Fish (Psari Skara)

In Greece fish is usually grilled over charcoal. Sometimes the fish is sprinkled with oregano before grilling.

2 pounds small whole fish
$^1/_2$ cup olive oil
juice of 1 to 2 lemons
salt to taste
parsley, chopped

Scrape, clean, and wash the fish. Sprinkle with salt and brush with oil. Place on a very hot grill. When the fish begins to brown, sprinkle with oil and lemon juice; turn and baste the other side. Turn again once or twice, until fish is cooked through. Place on a hot dish.

Beat oil, lemon juice, 1 tablespoon water, salt, and parsley. Pour over fish. Serve with tomato and cucumber salad. Enjoy! Makes 3 to 4 servings.

Tourcolimano-Style Shrimp

30 large shrimp
$^1/_2$ cup sherry wine
2 cloves garlic, chopped fine
6 ounces olive oil
3 medium onions, chopped fine
4 medium tomatoes, peeled and chopped

2 celery stalks, chopped fine
1 teaspoon thyme
1 teaspoon basil
salt and pepper
8 ounces feta, crumbled

Remove shrimp from shell, leaving the tails on. Devein shrimp and slit slightly. Place in a bowl and marinate with wine and garlic for 1 hour.

In a frying pan, heat olive oil. Add onions and saute until golden brown. Add chopped tomatoes, celery, thyme, basil, and season to taste with salt and pepper. Cook for 15 minutes over high heat.

In oval-shaped Pyrex dish, arrange shrimp in circular fashion with tails pointing outwards toward rim of dish. About six shrimp should fit in one dish.

Pour sauce over the shrimp, but not the tails. Sprinkle crumbled feta cheese over shrimp and sauce. Bake in 350° oven for 8 to 10 minutes. Rice pilaf and a glass of white wine make this a meal. Makes 5 servings.

Red Snapper in Mayonnaise (Psari Mayonnaisa)

While waiting for a fishing boat to dock, we heard the woes heaped on those sly fish-mongers who dripped blood on the eyes and gills of fish to make them appear fresher: they straightaway landed in jail! Against such deception, Greek people market with sharp eyes, looking for the characteristics of fresh fish: pink eyes, pink gills, firm scales and back, and a fresh sea smell. After cooking, a fresh fish emerges tender and suc-culent, with white, flaky meat and white bones. And in the city of New York people know and expect to buy "catch" fresh fish—period!

6 pounds whole fresh red snapper

juice of 2 lemons

2 tablespoons olive oil

3 bay leaves

$^1/_2$ teaspoon salt

6 small potatoes

Wash fish thoroughly in cold water; pat dry with a paper towel. Rub fish with salt and fresh lemon juice, including the cavity. Set aside for $^1/_2$ hour.

To cook fish, use a flat pot with a rack, or wrap the fish in a very porous, clean cheesecloth, and place fish flat in bottom of pot. Pour in enough hot water to barely cover the fish; add olive oil, bay leaves, and salt. Simmer 20 to 25 minutes, or until cooked. Carefully unwrap fish and gently place on a wide-lipped platter. Set aside to cool.

Boil 6 small potatoes, peel, and quarter. Place around fish in platter. Serve with may-onnaise. Makes 6 to 8 servings.

GARNISHES: Four hard-boiled eggs, sliced and placed all over fish. Arrange and dec-orate fish platter with black olives, sliced gherkins, radishes, chopped parsley, and grated nutmeg.

Baked Fish a la Parthenon (Psari Fournou a la Parthenon)

Pine forested Spetsai, the Saronic gulf island that guards the entrance to the Gulf of Argolikos, claims this dish as a specialty. It is also a feature of luxury cruise chefs in the Aegean.

3 pounds fish sliced 3/4-inch thick	1 cup olive oil
salt and pepper	3 onions, thinly sliced
juice of 1 lemon	2 cloves garlic, minced
2 cups fresh or canned tomatoes	2 tablespoons chopped parsley
1/2 cup white wine	dry bread crumbs

Wash fish and drain well. Sprinkle with salt, pepper, and lemon juice. Place in baking dish, set aside while preparing the sauce.

Combine remaining ingredients, except bread crumbs, in saucepan; cook 20 minutes. Spoon hot sauce over fish; sprinkle with bread crumbs. Bake uncovered in 350° oven for 45 minutes, basting twice with sauce. Makes an excellent first course with dry white wine. Makes 5 to 6 servings.

Baked Fish Mykonos (Psari Sto Fournou)

The people of the delightful sunbathed island of white Mykonos in the Aegean Sea prepare a delicious baked fish with aromatic herbs which is impossible to forget.

2 to 3 pounds whole fish (seasonal)

Marinade:

1/2 cup olive oil

juice of 2 lemons or 1/2 cup white wine

1 teaspoon salt

1/8 teaspoon pepper

1/4 teaspoon each: tarragon, rosemary, thyme,
and parsley

Wash, dry, and season fish with salt and pepper. Lay full length in shallow pan. Mix marinade well and ladle over fish. Let stand in refrigerator for 30 minutes. Turn over and marinate the other side for another 30 minutes. Spoon off some of the marinade to use as a basting sauce.

Bake 30 to 40 minutes, or until fork-tender, in a 350° oven. Allow 10 minutes per pound. Baste frequently with sauce while baking. Serve whole with garnishes such as black olives, feta cheese, or raw vegetables. Complement with a dry white Demestica wine. Makes 4 to 5 servings.

Fishmarket Catfish

The preparation of this recipe is simple, but the flavors you create are anything but simple. Savor the taste.

2 pounds catfish fillets

flour

salt and pepper

2 eggs, beaten

³/₄ cup vegetable oil

Demi-glace (brown sauce):

   2 cubes beef bouillon

   2¹/₂ cups boiling water

   2 sprigs parsley

   ¹/₄ cup butter or margarine

   6 tablespoons flour

   1 teaspoon soy sauce

Dill sauce:

   ¹/₄ cup butter

   1 tablespoon lemon juice

   ¹/₂ teaspoon chopped dill

   ¹/₄ cup brown sauce

Season flour with salt and pepper and dust fish fillets. Dip in eggs, then in flour. Heat vegetable oil until very hot. Add fish and saute, 4 to 5 minutes on each side, or until golden brown. Remove to heated platter.

To make demi-glace, dissolve bouillon cubes in boiling water and add parsley. Simmer 10 minutes. Remove parsley and return to boil. In a separate saucepan melt butter and stir in flour to make a thick paste. Add this mixture to boiling bouillon; add soy sauce and stir until glace has reached a medium consistency. Refrigerate extra demi-glace and serve, after reheating, as a garnish with other seafoods.

To make dill sauce, heat butter and lemon juice. Add dill. Stir in demi-glace. Cook and stir until heated through and blended.

Spoon dill sauce over fish fillets and garnish with lemon wedges and parsley. Makes 4 to 6 servings.

Baked Codfish with Tomatoes
(Bakaliaros Tou Fournou me Domates)

My dad introduced me to this excellent fish recipe. Dad said, "The initial preparation of codfish is most important. Rinse codfish well to remove salt. Cut into small pieces. Soak overnight in enough cold water to cover fish, changing the water five to six times." Dried salt codfish is most frequently used, although fresh cod may be substituted.

- 2 pounds dried cod
- 5 ripe tomatoes, peeled, seeded, and sliced
- 3 large potatoes, peeled and sliced into rounds
- 1/4 cup parsley, chopped
- 2 onions, thinly sliced
- 3 cloves garlic, minced
- 1/4 cup raisins
- 1 cup olive oil
- · pinch of salt and pepper

Remove and discard skin and bones from cod. Rinse cod well and drain; pat dry. Place half the tomato slices in a 9 x 13 inch baking pan. Add layers of fish, potatoes, parsley, onions, garlic, and raisins. Pour in half the olive oil. Add remaining tomato slices, and then rest of olive oil and salt and pepper. Bake uncovered in a 350° oven for 45 minutes. Makes 6 to 8 servings.

Fried Cod with Garlic Sauce
(Bakaliaros Tighanitos me Scorthali)

This delicious and frugal codfish recipe is served in most of your New York tavernas. Experience it!

- 1 pound dried cod (substitute fresh cod)
- 1 cup flour
- water (for batter mix)
- salt
- olive oil (for frying)

Cut fish into three 4-inch pieces. Soak overnight in cold water. Change water several times.

Remove skin and bones from fish. Place cod in saucepan with enough cold water to cover. Bring to boiling point. Remove from fire and leave to cool. Mix flour and water to make a thin batter; season with salt to taste. Heat oil in frying pan until hot. Oil must be hot enough to fry cod quickly. Dip cod in batter and fry quickly until golden brown on all sides. Cook only 3 to 4 pieces at a time. Serve piping hot with (skordalia) garlic sauce. Makes 2 to 3 servings.

Shrimp Casserole a la Roditys

The Kolpos, hundreds of bays which encompass the coastline of Greece, are the home of garithes, the best shrimp you'll ever eat. If you can't get to the Kolpos, I suggest you try this tasty dish instead.

1 **pound medium-sized raw shrimp**
2 **tablespoons butter**
3 **tomatoes, peeled and chopped**
1 **onion, chopped**
1 **clove garlic, minced**
1 **tablespoon brandy**
1 **tablespoon red wine**
¼ **pound feta cheese**
salt and pepper

Use a small sharp knife to pick off shell of shrimp. Slit shrimp down the back; clean off the black vein down the back of the shrimp. Rinse in cold water.

Bring one cup of water to a boil. Add shrimp, cover, and cook 1 minute. In a skillet, melt butter and add shrimp; cook over medium heat for 3 minutes or until shrimp are pink. Remove shrimp to a casserole dish. In skillet, add tomatoes, onions, and garlic and cook for 5 minutes. Add brandy, wine, and salt and pepper to taste; cook for 3 minutes longer. Pour sauce over shrimp and top with thin slices of feta cheese. Serve hot. Rice pilaf is a must! Makes 4 servings.

Squid in Wine (Kalamarakia Krassata)

This is a favorite dish throughout Greece and the surrounding islands. Greek cooks are adept at cleaning and cooking squid. If you don't like the fuss, then "Molfetas" Restaurant—the oldest restaurant in Manhattan—features this cuttle-fish.

2 **pounds cleaned squid**
2 **tablespoons salt**
¾ **cup olive oil**
½ **cup white wine**
4 **medium-sized tomatoes, peeled and diced**
pepper
chopped parsley
1 **lemon**

Wash squid in cold running water. Slit down the belly so that you can open into one piece. Remove the backbone, ink sac, and black skin. Rub with salt and wash again. Rinse thoroughly and pat dry.

Heat oil in a large-bottomed pan and saute squid. Add wine, tomatoes, parsley, and season with pepper to taste. Cook uncovered at low heat until squid is tender, about 1 hour. Serve cold with lemon wedges. Makes 5 to 6 servings.

Fried Mussels (Mythia Tiganita)

3 pounds mussels
1 to 2 eggs
4 to 5 tablespoons milk
1/3 cup flour
1 teaspoon baking powder
oil for frying
salt and pepper

Wash and scrub the mussels with a stiff brush, changing the water several times. Place in a large pot with 2 inches of water. Cover and cook until the shells open (about 8 minutes). Allow to cool; remove mussels from shells and drain.

Combine eggs and milk. Add flour and baking powder; mix well. Dip 2 or 3 mussels into the batter. Drop mussels into hot oil and fry until golden brown. Drain on paper towels and serve hot. Salt and pepper to taste. Garnish with lemon slices and parsley. Makes 4 to 6 servings.

Octopus in Wine (Oktapodi Tis Skaras)

A Greek fisherman will pound octopus against the rocks and spread its legs to dry out in the sun before it is grilled over hot coals.

This is the easy way to enjoy a dish that is very common and also appreciated in Greek tavernas in New York.

2 pounds octopus, skinned
2 onions, finely chopped
2 cloves garlic, minced
2 tablespoons parsley, chopped
2 bay leaves
1/2 teaspoon oregano
1/8 teaspoon thyme
1/4 cup olive oil
1 cup red wine
2 tablespoons fresh lemon juice
salt and pepper

Pound octopus until tender; cut into 2-inch cubes. Saute onions in olive oil until golden brown; add seasonings and continue to simmer. Add octopus and wine to onions and saute for 10 minutes. Add lemon juice to mixture. Add enough water to cover the octopus; cover and simmer for 1 1/2 hours or until octopus is tender. Serve hot with rice pilaf for a main course, or as an appetizer on a platter with lemon wedges and accompanied by crusty bread. Makes 4 servings.

Boiled Rock Lobster Tails (Astakos)

1   small onion, sliced
1   tablespoon salt
1/2 lemon, sliced
1   bay leaf
6   whole black peppercorns
5   (6-ounce) frozen rock lobster tails
2   tablespoons sherry wine

In a kettle, place 4 quarts water, onion, salt, lemon, bay leaf, and peppercorns; bring to boil.

With tongs, lower frozen lobster tails into boiling mixture. Return to a boil; reduce heat and simmer, covered for 9 to 10 minutes.

With tongs, remove lobster tails from kettle. Set aside until cool enough to handle. Discard the cooking liquid.

To remove meat from shells, use scissors to carefully cut away thin undershell. Insert fingers between shell and meat and gently pull meat. Cut lobster in bite-size pieces. Place in a bowl; sprinkle with sherry and serve warm. Makes 4 servings.

Fried Squid (Kalamarakia Tiganita)

2   pounds small squid
1   teaspoon salt
flour (for dredging)
olive oil (for frying)
lemon wedges

Clean squid as directed in Squid in Wine recipe (see page 76). Cut squid lengthwise, and cut again 1/2 inch horizontally. Season with salt. Dip in flour to coat, shake off excess flour. Heat oil in a frying pan and fry squid until golden brown. Serve with plenty of lemon wedges. Makes 4 servings.

Broiled Live Lobsters (Astakos)

Two popular types of lobsters are the Maine lobster, with the meat concentrated in the claws, and the spiny or rock lobster, with the meat coming mainly from the tail.
If you can't afford or find live lobsters, frozen lobster tails are easy to find and more reasonably priced.

1 **lemon, sliced thin**

1 **onion, sliced thin**

3 **bay leaves**

5 **tablespoons salt**

9 **whole black peppercorns**

2 **(1-pound) live lobsters**

melted butter

lemon wedges

In a deep kettle, combine 7 quarts water with lemon, onion, bay leaves, salt, and whole black peppercorns; bring to boil. Reduce heat and simmer, cover for 20 minutes.
Holding lobster by the body with tongs, claws away from you, plunge it into the boiling water. Repeat with second lobster. Bring to boil; reduce heat, cover kettle, and simmer lobster for 13 to 17 minutes.
Remove lobsters from kettle, place on their backs. Split body lengthwise, cutting through thin undershell, lobster meat, and back shell. Spread open. Remove and discard dark vein and small sac, which is below the head. Leave in green liver (tomalley) and red row (coral).
Crack large claws to let excess moisture drain. Serve lobsters at once with plenty of melted butter and lemon wedges. Makes 2 servings.

Baked Trout in Grape Leaves (Psari Fournou me Ambelophylla)

5 **whole trout (or any medium-sized fish)**

1/4 **cup olive oil**

juice of 1 large lemon

1 **tablespoon oregano**

1 **tablespoon chopped parsley**

1 **teaspoon salt**

1/4 **teaspoon pepper**

1 **8-ounce jar grape leaves**

olive oil (for brushing)

Clean trout and pat dry. In a bowl, combine 1/4 cup olive oil, lemon juice, parsley, oregano, salt, and pepper. Add the fish. Mix fish with all the ingredients in the bowl. Cover and marinate in the refrigerator for several hours.
Rinse grape leaves under running water thoroughly to remove the brine; pat dry. Drain the trout. Wrap each fish tightly in grape leaves. Use a large baking dish brushed with olive oil and place trout. Bake in a preheated 350° oven for 45 minutes. Do not turn. Place fish on a warm serving platter. Remove grape leaves before eating.

Codfish Baked with Currants (Bakaliaros Plaki)

6 slices fresh cod

2 medium onions, sliced thin

2 cloves garlic, minced

1/2 cup olive oil

juice of 1 lemon

1/2 cup currants, soaked in 1 cup of white wine

1 can whole tomatoes (16 ounces), chopped

3 whole cloves

4 tablespoons chopped parsley

salt and pepper to taste

Place cod slices on a slightly greased baking pan. Salt and pepper to taste. Rub cod slices with garlic, and pour lemon juice over fish. In a saucepan, lightly saute onions, parsley, and tomatoes; add currants, wine, and cloves, and simmer for 10 minutes. Pour this sauce over fish and bake in a preheated 400° oven for 45 minutes to 1 hour, basting the fish frequently. Serve a greek salad and crusty bread for dunking in the delicious sauce.

Cod Baked with Spinach and Garlic Sauce
(Bakaliaro me Spanaki)

6 cod steaks

2 bunches fresh spinach

1 bunch scallions, chopped

2 garlic cloves, minced

1/8 teaspoon oregano

juice of 1 lemon

1 cup garlic sauce (see page 66)

olive oil

Chop spinach. In a skillet, saute spinach, scallions, garlic, and oregano in 4 tablespoons of olive oil for 10 minutes. Place spinach mixtures in a baking pan slightly greased. Lay the cod steaks on the spinach. Pour lemon juice and 4 tablespoons olive oil over the cod steaks, and bake in a preheated oven at 350° for 45 minutes. Serve the cod steaks over a bed of spinach, and add garlic sauce on top. Serve a crusty Greek bread, and a glass of chilled white Retsina. A healthy dinner and frugal too!

MEATS

Braised Lamb (Kokkinisto Arni)

Besides being celebrities, Barbara Bush, Caesar Romero, Spiro Agnew, Paul Simon, Irv Kupcinet, Michael Bakalis, Len O'Conner, Jimmy the Greek, Elke Sommer, and Phyllis Diller share something else in common. They all love this dish.

3 pounds lamb, cut into serving pieces

3 ounces butter

1 large onion, chopped

1 bay leaf

2 cloves garlic, minced

$^1/_2$ glass white wine

salt and pepper to taste

Cut meat into uniform serving portions or walnut-sized cubes. Heat butter in a heavy braising pot and sear meat on all sides. Lower heat and add onions, cooking constantly until the onions soften. Gradually add wine and enough water to cover contents of pot. As the liquids begin to boil, lower the heat to simmer. Add salt, pepper, garlic, and bay leaf; cover and cook for 1 hour or until meat is very tender. Serve warm with feta cheese or yogurt, olives, crusty bread, and wine. Makes 6 servings.

NOTE: Each variation of Kokkinisto Arni is made with different vegetables. Most popular are green peas, okra, fresh beans, eggplant or artichokes. Care must be taken to add additional water for cooking pasta or vegetables and to see that the quick-cooking vegetables are added during the last 10 minutes, not before.

Lamb and Fresh Green Beans
(Arni Yahni me Freska Fasolakia)

Every Greek taverna serves this lamb favorite.

4 pounds lamb shoulder
1/4 cup vegetable oil
1 onion, chopped
3 cloves garlic, chopped
salt and pepper
4 bay leaves
6 whole allspice

2 ounces white wine
1 tomato, diced
3 tablespoons tomato paste, diluted in 10 ounces water
2 pounds fresh green beans
2 tablespoons parsley, chopped

Trim fat from lamb and cut in 4 pieces. In a large pot, heat vegetable oil until it begins to sizzle. Add lamb pieces and brown on all sides. In a small pot, saute onion and garlic until golden brown. Add onions to meat; salt and pepper to taste. Add bay leaves, allspice, white wine, and tomato. Mix well and cook over medium heat for 15 minutes. Add diluted tomato paste. If liquid does not cover all of the ingredients, add water. Cook for 2 hours over low heat.

Clean green beans and cook in separate pot with water for 15 minutes. Strain green beans and add to meat, along with chopped parsley. Cover pot and cook over medium heat for 1 hour longer, or until meat is tender. Serve with crusty bread. Makes 6 servings.

Lamb with Spinach Avgolemono (Arni me Spanaki Avgolemono)

Greeks still maintain their ancient tradition of eating lamb. It is cooked according to recipes that date back to the earliest days of recorded history. And this recipe is no exception.

1/4 cup butter	1 cup boiling water
3 tablespoons olive oil	2 pounds fresh spinach
2 1/2 pounds boneless lamb, cut in uniform size	1 teaspoon dill
2 onions, coarsely chopped	2 eggs
1 teaspoon salt	juice of 1 lemon
1/4 teaspoon pepper	

Heat butter and oil in a large pot. Add lamb pieces and brown on all sides. Add onions and saute until soft. Stirring, add salt, pepper, and boiling water. Simmer, covered, for 1 hour, adding water when necessary. While meat is simmering, wash spinach thoroughly and tear leaves into small pieces. In a separate pot, steam spinach until leaves are wilted, about 3 minutes. Remove and drain. Add spinach and dill to meat mixture. Stir and simmer for 15 minutes. Remove pot from heat.

Beat eggs until frothy. Slowly add lemon juice, beating constantly. Add 1 cup of liquid from meat mixture, at first slowly and then increasing the flow, beating constantly. Pour avgolemono sauce into the lamb and spinach and stir gently to combine. Serve hot with crusty bread for soaking. Makes 6 servings.

NOTE: If you wish, you may substitute romaine lettuce for spinach.

Lamb Saute with Orzo (Arni me Manestra)

Manestra, also known as orzo, is a pasta shaped like rice, but three times the size. It can be boiled and served buttered with cheese. This dish is a favorite throughout most of Greece, and in Manhattan's and Astoria's tavernas.

2 tablespoons olive oil	pepper to taste
1 pound lamb, cut into 2-inch cubes	1 teaspoon mint flakes
2 medium onions, chopped	4 cups boiling water
1 cup tomato sauce	1 cup orzo
1/8 teaspoon cinnamon	1 cup grated mizithra or parmesan cheese
1 teaspoon salt	

Heat oil in large saucepan and brown onions. Add lamb cubes and brown well on all sides. Add tomato sauce, 2 cups water, and seasonings. Cover and simmer for 1 hour or until lamb is tender. Add remaining 2 cups water and bring to a boil. Add orzo, stirring a few times. Simmer 20 to 25 minutes longer. Serve hot with grated cheese. Add a crisp salad, and red Retsina wine for a perfect meal. Makes 4 servings.

Lamb Stir Fry with Rice

I must admit that the Greek cuisine has finally taken a new approach in cooking their favorite—lamb.

3/4 pound boneless lamb, fat trimmed

cooking oil

1 tablespoon lemon juice

1/2 teaspoon each of oregano and rosemary, crushed

pepper to taste

1 clove garlic, minced

1 medium carrot, thinly bias-sliced

1 small onion, thinly sliced

1/2 pound fresh spinach, torn bite size

2 small tomatoes, cut in wedges

cooked white rice

Thinly slice lamb into 1 1/2-inch strips. Set aside.

In a small bowl combine 1 tablespoon oil, lemon juice, rosemary, oregano, and pepper. Mix well and set aside.

Place 1 tablespoon of oil in wok or skillet, stir fry garlic in hot oil for 25 seconds. Add carrots and onion; stir fry about 3 minutes or until crisp-tender.

Add 1 tablespoon additional oil. Add lamb; stir fry for 3 minutes or until done. Return vegetables to wok or skillet. Add lemon mixture; stir in spinach and tomatoes. Stir fry for 20 seconds. Remove from heat.

Serve over bed of rice. Top with crumbled feta cheese. A glass of Retsina wine goes well. Makes 3 servings.

Roast Leg of Lamb with Gravy (Arni Bouti Tou Fourno)

Taverna Vraka, 23–15 31st Street, features this roast lamb to perfection. This restaurant has been drawing New York celebrities for 25 years. It's said that Onassis and Governor Cuomo frequent the restaurant.

4- to 5-pound leg of lamb

salt and fresh ground pepper

2 cloves garlic, slivered

2 tablespoons butter, melted

juice of 1 lemon

$1/2$ cup water

1 cup hot water

2 tablespoons butter

2 tablespoons flour

Wipe off and dry leg of lamb and sprinkle with salt and pepper. Make 4 slits in the meat and insert garlic slivers.

Combine melted butter and lemon juice and brush over the lamb. Place meat on a rack in a shallow roasting pan, and add $1/2$ cup water. Insert a meat thermometer into the thickest portion of meat. Cover and bake in a preheated 325° oven for 1$1/2$ hours. Remove lid, increase the heat to 375°, and continue baking for 1$1/2$ hours longer, basting frequently (use meat thermometer to determine doneness). Transfer meat to a heated platter. Wrap leg in heavy tinfoil to keep warm.

To make gravy, skim fat from the pan drippings and discard. Add hot water to pan drippings and stir well. Melt butter in a small saucepan and blend in flour. Stir constantly until flour browns lightly. Strain liquid from pan and pour it into the browned flour, stirring until desired thickness. Pour into a gravy bowl and serve with lamb. Boiled greens and a glass of Roditis wine go well with this dish. Makes 6 to 8 servings.

Double Lamb Chop Wrapped in Flaky Pastry with Sun Dried Tomato Sauce

rack of lamb cut into double chops (6)

3 ounces olive oil

cracked black pepper, to taste

3 tablespoons roasted garlic puree

2 tablespoons minced shallots

4 ounces dried porcini mushrooms

2 ounces port wine

1/4 cup fresh chopped rosemary, thyme, sage, parsley (combined)

salt and pepper to taste

3 tablespoons pine nuts, lightly toasted

1/4 cup freshly grated parmesan

1 cup fresh breadcrumbs

olive oil (enough to moisten)

2 1/2 sticks melted butter

6 leaves filo dough

1 pint sun dried tomato sauce (see page 65)

Brush chops with oil and pepper and sear on grill or in a saute pan. Cool.

To prepare roasted garlic puree, place whole garlic in pan, brush with olive oil, sprinkle with thyme, and roast in oven at 350° for about 20 minutes. Remove garlic and puree.

To make stuffing: Saute shallots; add garlic puree, chopped mushrooms, herbs, port wine, pine nuts, parmesan cheese, and bread crumbs. Moisten with olive oil. Pack stuffing on and around rack of lamb.

Lay out 1 sheet of filo and brush with melted butter. Fold sheet in half and brush again. Fold in half again and brush with butter. Place lamb on filo and pull filo up and around lamb leaving the bone exposed. Brush with butter again and roast in a preheated 400° oven for about 25 minutes. Remove lamb from oven. Cut in half and serve with sun dried tomato sauce.

Lamb Chops Avgolemono

This tangy Greek recipe is an all-time Greek favorite—and understandably. It's a wonderful family affair. Simple to prepare, unusual, and very tasty.

1 **pound small new potatoes in their jackets**

2 **tablespoons olive oil**

6 **shoulder lamb chops**

3 **small stalks of celery, diced**

1 **large onion, diced**

1 **cup meat or chicken stock**

1 **egg**

juice of 1 lemon

1 **tablespoon cornstarch**

Boil the potatoes until tender; drain, set aside, and keep warm. In a large, heavy skillet, heat oil. Add lamb chops and brown quickly on both sides. Remove from the skillet, and set aside.

Saute celery and onions in the remaining fat in skillet until soft and translucent. Return lamb chops to skillet, placing on top of celery and onion. Pour the stock into the skillet; simmer, covered, for about 25 minutes. Remove from heat and keep covered while making sauce.

Beat egg until frothy. Beat in lemon juice and cornstarch. Transfer chops to heated serving platter and surround with the potatoes. Quickly bring the skillet juices back to boil. Add a spoonful of the hot juice to the egg-lemon mixture to warm it, then whisk mixture into skillet juices. Remove from heat immediately. Pour sauce over lamb and potatoes, and serve hot.

The sauce deserves a loaf of crusty bread for dunking. Add a tomato and onion salad with olive oil and vinegar, and a glass of wine. Makes 6 servings.

Greek Style Broiled Lamb Chops (Brizoles)

This is just one more lamb dish that I enjoy at Estia Taverna on East 86th street.

2 pounds baby lamb chops
1 tablespoon oregano
1 teaspoon mint flakes
$^{1}/_{2}$ teaspoon garlic powder (optional)
$^{1}/_{2}$ teaspoon thyme
1 teaspoon salt
pepper to taste
1 lemon

Mix herbs with salt and pepper in a small bowl. Preheat broiler at highest setting; high heat is needed to broil quickly so that chops remain tender. Arrange chops on unslotted broiler pan. Sprinkle and rub herb mixture on both sides of chops. Broil chops for 8 minutes; turn over and sprinkle tops with remaining herb mixture. Continue broiling 6 to 8 minutes more, depending on desired doneness. Remove chops to a serving platter and squeeze half a lemon over them. Serve with a small Greek salad and Greek bread. Makes 4 servings.

Pork chops can be used in place of lamb chops.

Broiled Lamb Chops (Paidakia Tis Scaras)

Lamb chops do not have to take long to prepare. Lamb shoulder chops are made quick, moist, and very tasty.

The Greek restaurants in New York prepare this dish perfectly.

4 lamb shoulder chops

3 tablespoons melted butter

juice of 1 lemon

1 garlic clove, minced

1 teaspoon oregano

salt and pepper

Combine melted butter, lemon juice, garlic, and oregano. Season chops with salt and pepper, and baste with lemon juice mixture. Place chops on a rack in broiler with a dripping pan. Broil chops on both sides, basting several times until the lemon juice mixture is gone. Serve at once, spooning hot pan drippings over chops. Accompany with boiled greens with olive oil or sliced tomatoes, oregano, and a glass of Boutari Roditis wine. Makes 4 servings.

Lamb and Leek Stew (Arni me Prassa)

Lamb is the staple meat of Greece and is traditionally served with pilaf. Next to the leg, lamb shanks are the best cut, as they offer the most meat with the least fat.

2 lamb shanks

1 tablespoon butter

3 ounces tomato paste

1 teaspoon salt

pepper to taste

3 or 4 leeks or 2 bunches scallions

$1/2$ cup orzo

Trim fat from lamb shanks. Cut meat from bones into $1^{1}/2$-inch cubes, saving bones. Melt butter in dutch oven. Brown lamb on all sides. Add 4 cups of water, tomato paste, salt, pepper, and bones. Bring to a boil. Cover and simmer for $1^{1}/4$ hours.

Wash and trim leeks well. Cut into $1/2$-inch slices using most of green part. (If scallions are used, cut into 1-inch slices.)

Remove bones from pot and add leeks. Simmer covered for 15 minutes. Add orzo and simmer 15 minutes longer, stirring often to prevent sticking. Serve with crusty bread. Makes 2 to 4 servings.

Lamb Stew with Tomato (Kokkinisto Arni me Domates)

This recipe originated on the Peloponnesus Peninsula and has carried its flavor throughout New York's Greek tavernas. My choice for this delicious stew is Avegerino's at 153 East 53rd Street.

2 1/2 pounds lean lamb
flour
1/2 cup olive oil
1 medium onion, chopped
2 cloves garlic, minced
1 tablespoon fresh parsley, chopped
1 teaspoon mint flakes
1 teaspoon dill
1 teaspoon basil
1 teaspoon thyme
2 bay leaves

1/2 teaspoon clove
1 teaspoon cinnamon
2 large tomatoes, peeled and chopped
4 ribs celery, chopped
4 large carrots, chopped
1/2 cup red wine, dry
1/4 cup sugar
pepper to taste

Cut meat into uniform 1-inch cubes, dredge in flour.
Heat oil in a deep pot and sear meat on all sides. Add onions and garlic; cook until onions are soft. Add herbs, stirring constantly. Cover pot and remove from heat. In a small pot mix tomatoes, carrots, and celery. Cook over medium heat 5 minutes, until vegetables are hot. Add vegetables to meat mixture. Add wine, sugar, and water to cover meat and vegetables. Bring mixture to boil; cover, reduce heat, and simmer for 1 to 1 1/2 hours, or until meat is tender. Season with pepper. Serve with cooked white rice or orzo. Makes 6 to 8 servings.

Lamb Stew (Arni Kapama)

This is another dish I've enjoyed—at Uraka and Zenon Tavernas, located on 31st Avenue in Astoria. They serve quality, well-seasoned food.

2 tablespoons butter

2 lamb shanks, fat trimmed off

1 medium onion, chopped

3 1/2 cups water

1/2 can (6 ounces) tomato paste

dash allspice, cinnamon, and nutmeg

1 teaspoon salt

pepper to taste

2 or 3 potatoes

1 package (10 ounces) French cut green beans

Heat butter in a large dutch oven. Brown shanks on all sides. Add onion, and saute until soft. Add 3 1/2 cups water and bring to boil. Cover and simmer for 1 1/4 hours. Refrigerate to cool and allow fat to harden. Remove fat and reheat lamb.

Peel potatoes and cut into eighths. Add tomato paste, spices, salt, pepper, and potatoes to lamb. Simmer 20 minutes, or until potatoes are almost done. Add green beans and simmer 10 minutes longer or until done. Adjust salt to taste. Serve with crusty bread for soaking.

NOTE: One 10-ounce package of peas or brussels sprouts, or 1 pound fresh zucchini sliced 1/4-inch thick may be substituted for green beans. Add zucchini slices along with potatoes. Makes 2 to 4 servings.

Baked Lamb and Potatoes (Youvetsi me Patates)

Periyali, located at 35 West 20th Street, serves lamb dishes that are worth the decibel level. This baked lamb with youvetsi potatoes is outstanding.

1/2 cup butter

2 1/2 pounds boneless lamb (cut into 2-inch cubes)

2 onions, thinly sliced

2 cloves garlic, minced

1 teaspoon salt

1/2 teaspoon pepper

1 can (10 ounces) tomato sauce

2 pounds potatoes, peeled and quartered

Melt butter in a large baking dish or roasting pan. Add lamb, onions, and garlic; stir until coated with butter. Sprinkle with salt and pepper.

Preheat oven to 450° and bake uncovered until meat is browned on all sides, about 30 minutes. Reduce temperature to 325° and add tomato sauce. Bake for 45 minutes longer. Add boiling water if necessary.

Add potatoes to roasting pan and spoon pan juices over them to coat them well. Bake until potatoes are done, about 3/4 of an hour longer. Serve boiled endive and olive oil for a meal. Makes 4 to 5 servings.

Peasant Style Baked Lamb (Horiatiko)

James Gekas, my dad, is the author of this tasty lamb dish. Dad says, "Do not turn the meat but baste from time to time."

2 **pounds breast or lamb shoulder**

salt and pepper to taste

2 **pounds tomatoes, peeled and sliced**

1 **pound feta cheese**

2 **tablespoons olive oil**

Wash lamb in cold water and pat dry with paper towel. Cut lamb into large pieces. Salt and pepper to taste. Peel and slice tomatoes and place over top of lamb. Cut feta cheese into small pieces and arrange over lamb. Pour olive oil over lamb.

Bake at 325° for 1½ hours or until meat is tender. Do not turn meat, but baste frequently. Garlic can also be added to this dish if desired. Vegetables, rice, or macaroni go well with this lamb dish. Serve with a glass of Mt. Ambellos dry wine. Makes 4 servings.

Greek Meatballs (Keftedes)

5 **pieces sliced bread, crusts removed**

3 **pounds ground round steak**

1 **cup chopped parsley**

1 **large onion, grated**

2 **eggs, beaten**

1 **tablespoon mint leaves**

salt and pepper

corn oil

juice of 1 lemon

Moisten bread in water and squeeze out any excess water. In a large bowl, combine bread, meat, parsley, onion, eggs, mint, and season to taste with salt and pepper. Mix well. With floured hands form meatballs two inches in diameter. Heat oil in a large frying pan over medium-high heat. Add meatballs, a few at a time, and brown on all sides; remove from pan when browned. After all the meatballs have been fried, discard all drippings and oil from frying pan. Return meatballs to pan; squeeze juice of lemon over meatballs. Cover with lid to keep warm. Serve with boiled greens and white rice or pilaf. Yields 48 meatballs.

Meatballs with Rice Avgolemono
(Youvarlakia Avgolemono)

Manhattan's tavernas have just added one more recipe to my cookbook. The meatballs are so tasty and soft. How could I refuse the sauce? Have plenty of crusty bread for soaking.

1 pound ground beef	salt and pepper
⅓ cup rice	½ cup flour
1 egg, beaten	Sauce:
1 clove garlic, minced	1 cup boiling chicken broth or bouillon
2 tablespoons parsley, chopped	
2 tablespoons fresh dill, chopped or 2 teaspoons dried dill	2 eggs
	juice of 1 lemon

Combine meat, rice, egg, garlic, parsley, dill, and salt and pepper to taste. Knead well. Shape in walnut-size balls. Roll them lightly in flour. Shake off excess flour.

Place meatballs in 4-quart casserole dish. Pour in enough boiling chicken broth to cover. Simmer covered for 45 minutes. Add broth (or water) if there is less than 1 cup of liquid left. Boil a few minutes more and remove pot from heat.

Beat 2 eggs until frothy. Slowly add the juice of one lemon, beating continuously. Add a cup of pot liquid, at first drop by drop and slowly increasing, while beating constantly. Pour avgolemono sauce into the pot of meatballs. With a wooden spoon, stir gently. Serve hot. Makes 24 meatballs.

Greek Style Meatloaf

There's more to meatloaf than meets the blue-plate special. Just ask anyone who makes it or remembers eating it the way Mom made it (the only way, of course), and you'll get advice on the best way to make it.

You have to be careful when you make a flavored meatloaf. If it's too seasoned, it can kill the character of the meatloaf. Then you are creating something else.

2^1/$_2$ pounds ground chuck

^{1}/$_2$ pound finely diced feta cheese

10 pitted black olives, chopped

1 small onion, peeled and diced

1 tablespoon oregano

1 tablespoon ground cumin

1 tablespoon paprika

1 teaspoon black pepper

1^1/$_2$ teaspoons salt

1 tablespoon garlic powder

1 egg

^{1}/$_2$ cup bread crumbs

In a large bowl, mix all the ingredients thoroughly. In a jelly-roll pan, shape meat into a loaf, making sure there are no bubbles. Wet hands for easier and firmer shaping.

Bake in a preheated 350° oven for 1 hour, or until the temperature registers 165° on a meat thermometer. If meat seems to be browning too quickly, cover with foil. Remove from oven; let meatloaf stand for 15 minutes to firm up. Slice and serve with mashed potatoes and gravy. Makes 8 servings.

Greek Style Hamburger (Kefta Sti Skara)

No one prepares a Greek hamburger like Greek tavernas. I'm told that a shot of ouzo mixed into the meat mixture can make all the difference.

1 pound lean ground beef
1 teaspoon spearmint
1 teaspoon oregano
1 small onion, chopped fine
1 egg, beaten lightly
1 slice white bread, discard crust
2 ounces red wine
2 tablespoons water
salt and pepper

In a bowl, combine meat, spearmint, oregano, and onion; mix well. Soak bread in wine and add to meat mixture. Salt and pepper to taste. Add lightly beaten egg and water; mix well. Divide mixture into 4 equal portions; lightly shape each portion into a patty ¾ to 1 inch thick. Broil or grill to desired doneness. Makes 4 servings.

Meatballs a la Smyrna (Keftaides Tou Fournou)

Every taverna in New York has a variation of this dish. So tasty!

2 pounds ground beef
2 onions, chopped fine
2 sprigs of parsley, chopped
2 cloves garlic, minced
salt and pepper
1 egg, beaten
2 tablespoons tomato paste diluted in 8 ounces of water
4 ounces vegetable oil
4 bay leaves

In a large bowl, add ground beef, one onion, parsley, garlic, and salt and pepper to taste. Add beaten egg and knead well.

In a large frying pan, saute second onion in oil until soft and transparent. Add diluted tomato paste and cook for 15 minutes. With floured hands form meatballs 3 inches long and 1½ inches wide (oval shape). In a second frying pan, heat oil and cook meatballs, turning to brown on all sides. Place meatballs in a baking pan. Add bay leaves to onion mixture and pour over meatballs. Cover with aluminum foil and bake in 350° oven for 1 hour. Uncover and continue to bake until meatballs have a brownish-red color. Serve over a bed of rice pilaf. Makes 24 meatballs.

Greek Style Meat Pie

The meat should be cut into very small pieces or ground coarsely, not as fine as hamburger. Make sure that your phyllo pastry is thoroughly thawed before using.

2 sticks sweet butter

3 pounds beef (see above)

1 onion, chopped

1 tablespoon tomato paste, diluted in 1 cup water

2 cloves garlic, slivered thin

2 tablespoons parsley, chopped

1 teaspoon fresh mint, chopped

$1/2$ pound kefalotiri cheese, grated

2 eggs, lightly beaten

salt and pepper

2 hard-boiled eggs, crumbled

18 sheets phyllo pastry

Melt $2/3$ stick of butter. Add onion and meat and cook until lightly brown. Add diluted tomato paste to meat mixture. Add garlic, parsley, mint, and salt and pepper to taste. Mix well and simmer for $1/2$ hour.

Remove from heat and add cheese and beaten eggs. Mix well. Melt the remaining butter and set aside for brushing pastry.

Butter a 13 x 9 baking pan. Place 9 phyllo sheets on bottom of pan, and brush phyllo sheets with melted butter. Do not trim the sheets; let excess go up sides of the pan. Pour meat mixture over the phyllo sheets and spread crumbled eggs over top. Fold the overhanging edges of the phyllo sheets over the top of the filling and brush them with melted butter. Place remaining 9 phyllo sheets on top, buttering each sheet. Score the top lightly with a sharp knife to indicate servings. Bake in a 325° oven for 1 hour until phyllo is golden brown. Let meat pie stand for 30 minutes before cutting. Makes 10 to 12 servings.

Light Moussaka

This recipe is just what the doctor ordered—low in fat, but high in nutritional value. And it still retains the taste and appearance of the original Greek recipe.

2 large unpeeled eggplants cut into $1/4$-inch slices (about 2 pounds)

vegetable cooking spray

$3/4$ teaspoon garlic powder

1 pound ground chuck

$1/2$ cup chopped onions

1 cup chablis or other white wine

1 (8-ounce) can no-salt-added tomato sauce

2 tablespoons minced fresh parsley

$1/2$ teaspoon black pepper

$1/4$ teaspoon salt

$1/8$ teaspoon ground nutmeg

White sauce:

1 (12-ounce) can evaporated skim milk

$1/2$ cup low-sodium chicken broth

$1/4$ cup all-purpose flour

$1/8$ teaspoon white pepper

$1/4$ cup grated parmesan cheese

Arrange eggplant slices in a single layer on a baking sheet coated with cooking spray. Coat top surface of eggplant with cooking spray and sprinkle with garlic powder. Bake at 425° for 15 minutes or until lightly browned. Set aside.

Combine ground chuck and onion in a large nonstick skillet; cook over medium heat until browned, stirring to crumble. Drain and pat dry with paper towels. Wipe pan drippings from skillet with paper towel. Return meat mixture to skillet; add wine and next 5 ingredients. Cook 15 minutes, stirring occasionally. Remove from heat; let cool.

In a bowl combine milk and chicken broth; set aside. Combine flour and white pepper in a saucepan. Gradually add milk mixture, stirring with a wire whisk until smooth. Stirring frequently, cook over medium heat for 10 minutes, or until thickened.

Arrange $1/3$ of eggplant in the bottom of a 12 x 8 x 2-inch baking dish; top with $1/3$ of meat mixture. Spread $1/3$ of white sauce over meat, and top with $1/3$ of cheese. Repeat procedure with remaining eggplant, meat mixture, white sauce, and cheese.

Bake at 350° for 30 minutes or until moussaka is thoroughly heated. Serve with crusty bread, a salad made with romaine lettuce, and dry white wine. Makes 6 to 8 servings. Only 295 calories per serving.

Baked Eggplant Moussaka (Moussaka)

The most famous eggplant recipe in all the Near East is called moussaka. Though the origin is not known for certain, the recipe was probably carried to Greece by the Arabs when they introduced the eggplant in the Middle Ages.

My brother John, owner of the Palomino Restaurant in Tucson, introduced this elegant dish to his eggplant lovers thirty years ago. John is gone, but his son, Jimmy, has continued the tradition of preparing super Greek creations, especially during the winter months for his New York visitors. Yiasou Jim!

3 eggplants

vegetable oil

1 cup chopped onions

2 pounds ground beef

1 (8-ounce) can tomato paste, diluted in 1 cup water

1 cup dry white wine

salt and pepper

$1/4$ teaspoon nutmeg

2 tablespoons chopped parsley

1 cup dry bread crumbs

1 cup grated kefalotiri or parmesan cheese

White sauce:

$1/8$ pound butter

1 cup flour

1 quart milk, heated

3 eggs, beaten

$1/2$ cup grated parmesan cheese

Peel and slice eggplant into $1/4$ inch thick slices. Salt well on both sides of slices. Let stand for 1 hour; rinse in cold water and drain. Heat oil in frying pan and add eggplant. Cook for 3 to 4 minutes. Remove from pan and drain on absorbent paper. In separate pan, saute onion in butter. Add meat and cook until well browned. Add diluted tomato paste, wine, nutmeg, parsley, and season to taste with salt and pepper. Simmer until ingredients are well blended.

To make white sauce, melt butter in saucepan. Add flour gradually, stirring until well blended. Add heated milk and stir until thickened. Stir in well beaten eggs, nutmeg, and salt and pepper to taste. Cook for 1 minute, stirring constantly. Add cheese and stir until melted into sauce.

Sprinkle bread crumbs on the bottom of 13 x 9 baking dish. In layers, add $1/2$ of eggplant, $1/2$ of meat mixture, $1/3$ of cheese, and then $1/3$ of bread crumbs. Repeat layers. Pour on white sauce and top with remaining cheese and bread crumbs. Bake at 350° for $1/2$ hour or until golden brown. Cool slightly before cutting. Makes 10 servings.

Au Jus Pan Gravy (Saltsa)

It takes a Greek to know what to do with natural drippings of juices from baked, broiled, or fried meats, fowl, or fish.
Crusty bread is the best way to enjoy dipping in this gravy.

> **juice of 1 lemon**
> **1/2 cup boiling water**
> **dash salt and pepper to taste**

After removing cooked meat, fish, or fowl from pan, add above ingredients to the drippings and return to fire for 3 to 4 minutes. Pour it over your meats or serve it in bowls with crusty bread for dipping.

Steak a la Greque (Sofrito)

The brave guerillas were served this steak when they claimed victory over the Turks. Today it's popular all over Greece and a favorite at most New York tavernas.

> **2 1/2 pounds round steak**
> **1/2 cup flour**
> **salt and pepper**
> **oil (for cooking)**
> **2 cloves garlic, sliced thin**
> **1 cup dry red wine**
> **1 cup water**
> **1 teaspoon sugar**

Cut round steak into 5 portions and pound steak with mallet until thin. Flour both sides of meat and salt and pepper to taste.
Heat oil in a large frying pan. Brown meat 5 to 7 minutes on both sides. Add remaining ingredients. Bring to a boil. Cover and simmer for 1 1/2 hours. Serve with boiled horta and crusty bread. Makes 5 servings.

Cabbage Dolmathes (Lahanodolmades)

Balkan influences filtered into Greek cuisine through Macedonia as well as Epirus. Some Macedonians use caraway in their stuffed cabbage. You will need extra crusty bread to soak up that delicious lemon sauce. Delightful!

1   head cabbage

1   pound ground beef

1   onion, chopped finely

1   egg, beaten lightly

$1/2$ cup rice

$1/4$ cup parsley, chopped

$1/2$ cup tomato sauce

$1/2$ teaspoon salt

pepper to taste

egg and lemon sauce (see page 64)

Cut out core from cabbage head. Drop the whole cabbage into boiling water and cook for 10 to 15 minutes. Remove cabbage leaves, one by one. Spread out on a counter.

For filling, combine ground beef, onions, egg, rice, parsley, tomato sauce, salt, and pepper. Knead well.

Place two tablespoons of filling on each cabbage leaf, near the end of the stem. Fold leaf over from right, and then from left, towards the center. Pick up stem and roll away from you, as snug as possible, covering filling with all the leaf. The rolls should have the same shape as a large egg roll.

In a large skillet, pack rolls snugly side by side. Add water to cover rolls. Cover and bring to a boil; reduce heat and simmer for 45 minutes.

Prepare avgolemono sauce as directed on page 64. Add the hot cooked liquid drop by drop. Heat without boiling and pour over stuffed cabbage. Makes 5 servings.

Pastitsio

A pastitsio recipe that calls for no bechamel sauce and is enclosed with phyllo pastry is preferred by many cooks in this country. I enjoy making pastitsio with cream sauce, and I do hope you will be pleased with the outcome. Experience it!

1 stick butter	1 pound macaroni
2 pounds ground beef, lean	1 cup romano cheese, grated
2 onions, chopped (1 cup)	4 eggs, beaten
1 clove garlic, minced	1/2 stick melted butter
1/2 cup water	Cream sauce:
1 tablespoon salt	1/2 stick butter
1/4 teaspoon nutmeg	1/2 cup romano cheese, grated
1/4 teaspoon allspice	1 pint half and half cream
1/4 teaspoon cinnamon	1 cup flour
1 can (6 ounces) tomato paste	4 cups milk
white pepper to taste	6 eggs, beaten
1/2 cup dry white wine	

Heat butter and brown beef. Then push beef to one side of the frying pan and add onion and garlic and saute until soft. Stir onion and meat together. Add water and salt. Cook until water is absorbed. Add nutmeg, allspice, and cinnamon; mix well. Add tomato paste and dry white wine. Simmer till all liquids are absorbed. Sprinkle with pepper to taste. Set aside.

Cook macaroni in salted water according to the directions on package. Drain, rinse, drain again, and place in bowl. Mix with melted butter and cheese; stir in beaten eggs. Add macaroni and meat mixture; blend well.

For cream sauce, melt butter in saucepan. Add cheese, flour, cream, and milk. Cook over low flame, stirring constantly until thick. Remove from heat and cool slightly. Add beaten eggs and mix well.

Stir in 1/2 of cream sauce with macaroni and meat mixture, and mix well. Fold mixture into 10 x 14 x 2 1/2 pan. Pour remaining cream sauce on top. Sprinkle top with cinnamon and nutmeg. Bake at 350° for 45 minutes. Remove from oven, let cool for 1/2 hour before cutting. Goes great with a fresh garden salad. Serves 12 as a main course.

Greek Style Grilled Liver (Skoti Tiganito)

Restaurant managers in New York suggest this dinner along with Greek wine. This liver preparation is simple and will give you a new image of liver.

1/4 cup olive oil

1   clove garlic, crushed

1   tablespoon oregano, crushed

salt and pepper to taste

1   pound calf liver or baby beef liver, sliced thin

juice of 1 lemon

Combine first four ingredients. Marinate liver in mixture for 30 minutes. Cook liver on a hot grill for 10 minutes, turning once. Take caution not to overcook, or liver will be tough. Squeeze lemon over liver and serve hot. Makes 3 servings.

Beef Stew (Kapama)

Beef stew is an American dish, but by adjusting the spices you have a Greek version. Go for it!

2 1/2 pounds beef for stew (lean boneless beef chuck)

3   tablespoons butter

1   large onion, chopped

4 to 5 medium potatoes, pared and quartered

1   can (6 ounces) tomato paste

1/4 teaspoon allspice

1/4 teaspoon nutmeg

1/4 teaspoon cinnamon

salt and pepper to taste

2   packages (10 ounces) frozen French cut string beans, defrosted

Cut beef into 1-inch pieces. Heat butter in a dutch oven. Add beef cubes and cook over medium heat until cubes are well browned on all sides. Remove meat as browned. Add onion to drippings; saute until tender and golden brown—about 10 minutes. Return meat to dutch oven with onions. Add enough water to just cover meat. Bring to a boil; reduce heat, and simmer for 1 hour and 25 minutes. Add potatoes, tomato paste, spices, and salt and pepper to taste. Cook for 20 minutes, or until potatoes are almost done. Add string beans; simmer 10 minutes, or until done. Serve with crusty bread for soaking. Makes 6 servings.

Beef Stew with Onions (Stifatho)

The Irish have their wonderful Irish stew, and the Greeks have their "stifatho," a hearty stew that goes well with cool weather.

4   tablespoons vegetable oil

2   pounds top round meat, cut into 2-inch cubes

3   cups thinly sliced onions

2   cloves garlic, finely sliced

1   can (6 ounces) tomato paste

1   can (10$^{1}/_{2}$ ounces) beef broth

1   cup water

$^{1}/_{4}$ cup red wine vinegar

$^{1}/_{4}$ teaspoon cinnamon

1   bay leaf, whole

salt and pepper

In a dutch oven, heat oil until it begins to sizzle. Add meat and brown on all sides. When meat is browned, remove with a slotted spoon and set aside. Put onions and garlic in a dutch oven and cook until lightly brown. Return meat to dutch oven and add tomato paste, beef broth, water, vinegar, cinnamon, and bay leaf. Salt and pepper to taste and mix well. Cover dutch oven and simmer for 2$^{1}/_{2}$ to 3 hours, until meat is very tender and the sauce is thick. Stir occasionally so meat won't stick to the dutch oven. Remove bay leaf and serve. To vary this savory dish, add 6 ounces of crumbled feta cheese before serving. Makes 6 servings.

Pork Chops Village Style (Brizzoles Tou Hirinou)

When Greeks get together they must drink. And when drinking they must eat. This is a traditional dish found in the tavernas in the heart of Corfu, away from the tourist beaches, where old traditions of living and eating still flourish.

4 large pork chops, on or off the bone

juice of $^{1}/_{2}$ large lemon

$^{2}/_{3}$ cup oil

1 teaspoon salt

1 teaspoon oregano

$^{1}/_{2}$ teaspoon pepper

Mix all ingredients together in a bowl and marinate chops for three to four hours in the refrigerator. If possible, allow chops to marinate overnight. Remove meat and let it drain on a plate for 10 minutes. Grill chops on a barbecue, or cook in the oven or broiler, basting them occasionally with marinade and turning them once. Serve with boiled greens, and a bowl of feta cheese. Makes 4 servings.

Pork Chops and Celery Avgolemono
(Hirino me Selino Avgolemono)

The best of Greek cuisine is not necessarily difficult.

- 4 medium pork chops
- 1 medium onion, finely chopped
- 2 tablespoons butter
- 3 stalks celery, diced
- 1 chicken boullion cube

salt and pepper

- 1 egg, beaten lightly

juice of 1 lemon

- 1 tablespoon cornstarch

Melt butter in frying pan. Add pork chops and quickly sear on both sides; remove from frying pan. Saute onion and celery until soft. In a bowl, dissolve boullion in 1 cup hot water. Place chops on top of onions and celery, adding boullion over chops. Sprinkle with salt and pepper to taste. Cover and simmer for 45 minutes. Remove from heat, placing chops on plate.

Prepare avgolemono sauce: Beat egg until slightly foamy and light yellow. Dilute cornstarch in $1/4$ cup water and add to the egg. Add lemon juice, and beat well. Stir a ladleful of pan juice from the meat to the egg-and-lemon mixture, beating it in thoroughly. Stir this mixture back into pan. Stir over medium heat for several minutes, until sauce thickens. Spoon sauce over chops. With this lemon sauce you need a loaf of crusty bread. Makes 4 servings.

Pork with Cabbage (Hirino me Lahano)

Choose a boneless pork roast that has little fat and the results will be juicy and have excellent flavor.

Don't take this dish lightly just because it is so simple to prepare. The best of Greek cuisine is not necessarily complex.

$^1/_2$ cup olive oil

2 $^1/_2$ pounds lean pork, cut into 1-inch cubes

2 onions, thinly sliced

1 can (10 ounces) tomato sauce

3 tablespoons red wine vinegar

1 teaspoon salt

pepper to taste

1 cup boiling water

2 heads cabbage (medium size)

Heat olive oil in frying pan and brown pork on all sides. Push pork to side of pan and saute onions until soft. Stir onions and pork together. Add tomato sauce, vinegar, salt, and pepper. Cook 3 to 4 minutes longer. Add boiling water, cover, and simmer for 1 hour, or longer. Check every 30 minutes and add boiling water if necessary.

Towards the end of cooking time, cut your cabbage into strips, add to pork, and cook until pork and cabbage are tender and sauce has thickened, about 30 minutes longer. Makes 5 to 6 servings.

Miniature Pork Kebabs (Hirines Souvlakia)

We Americans are funny. We will work long and hard to make meat dishes taste good. Here's one that is easy to prepare. Ask your butcher for a pork tenderloin strip, and the rest is easy.

If time is of essence—get over to Zygos Taverna in Astoria. Let their cooks prepare their version of pork tenderloin in their special way: broiled on a skewer with wedges of onions, tomatoes, and green peppers.

1 pound lean pork tenderloin, cut in 1-inch cubes

8 tablespoons olive oil

$^1/_2$ teaspoon thyme

$^1/_2$ teaspoon paprika

$^1/_2$ teaspoon minced parsley

1 bay leaf, crumbled

$^1/_2$ teaspoon ground red pepper

salt and pepper

Combine all ingredients except pork cubes; mix well. Add pork cubes to marinade. Cover and refrigerate 4 to 6 hours. Thread pork cubes on small skewers. Broil until well browned. Baste several times while broiling. Serve over a bed of rice, with a tossed salad. Makes 4 servings.

Smyrna-Style Shish Kebabs

Credit for shish kebabs is commonly given to the Turkish. But, about 500 B.C., the Greeks used a shallow clay brazier, called an eschara, with lugs at either side so the spits could be turned easily to broil the meat.

This recipe is from Georgette Kontos, who operates and teaches at St. Haralambos Regional Cooking School in Niles, Illinois. Georgette is an exciting cook and an excellent teacher.

2$^1/_2$ pounds pork tenderloin

1 cup dry red wine

$^1/_2$ tablespoon oregano

$^1/_2$ tablespoon thyme

$^1/_2$ tablespoon minced garlic

$^3/_4$ to 1 cup fresh lemon juice

2 to 3 medium onions, chopped

$^3/_4$ cup virgin olive oil

salt and pepper

Cut pork into 1$^1/_2$- to 2-inch cubes. Combine wine, oregano, thyme, garlic, lemon juice to taste, onions, and oil in a glass or ceramic container. Season with salt and pepper to taste. Place pork cubes in marinade. Cover and refrigerate for 10 hours, or as long as 2 days.

Remove pork from marinade. Thread pork cubes on skewers; reserve marinade.

Grill skewers 4 inches from preheated oven broiler for 10 minutes, or over ash-covered coals, until they reach desired degree of doneness, basting frequently with marinade. Makes 6 to 8 servings.

Lamb with Fresh Vegetables (Arni me Lahaneka)

This popular lamb casserole is a favorite in all of New York metropolitan tavernas.

3 to 4 pounds boneless lamb stew
5 tablespoons butter
1¹/₂ cups onion, chopped fine
1 cup hot water
1¹/₂ cups tomato sauce
¹/₄ cup chopped parsley
1 head cabbage (large)
salt and pepper to taste

Cut lamb into 2- to 3-inch pieces.
Melt butter in large casserole. Add lamb and onions and brown well over moderate heat. Add tomato sauce, hot water, salt and pepper, and parsley. Add cabbage, cut in wedges, and cook covered for 45 minutes or until lamb is tender. Add more water if needed.

NOTE: Celery or dandelion greens may be substituted for cabbage.

Lamb Shanks and Artichoke Hearts Avgolemono
(Arni me Anginares)

2 lamb shanks
2 tablespoons butter
1 onion, finely chopped
salt and pepper to taste
2 tablespoons fresh parsley (chopped)
1 can or 1 package frozen artichoke hearts, drained
2 eggs
juice of 2 lemons
2 tablespoons cornstarch

Trim fat from lamb shanks. In a dutch oven, brown well in butter. Add onion and saute until soft. Add 2¹/₂ cups water, salt, and pepper. Bring to boil. Cover and simmer 1¹/₂ hours or until lamb is tender. Turn shanks occasionally. Add water if necessary. Add parsley and artichoke hearts. Cook 5 minutes (15 minutes if frozen). Adjust salt. Remove from heat. Make avgolemono sauce: Beat eggs with a wisk until slightly foamy. Add lemon and cornstarch. Beat again. Stir a ladleful of lamb stock into the bowl of avgolemono. Gently stir this mixture back in the pot. Stir over low heat until sauce thickens. Rice pilaf goes well, as does crusty bread for soaking up this delicious sauce!

Stuffed Zucchini (Papoutsakia)

Papoutsakia means "little shoes." This long Greek word may mean "little shoes"—but it sure will feed 5 grown-ups in a hurry!

5   zucchini, uniform size
3   tablespoons chopped parsley
1   clove garlic, minced
1   medium onion, chopped fine
$^1/_2$ teaspoon oregano
$^1/_3$ pound ground beef
salt and pepper to taste
butter
3   tablespoons dry white wine
bechamel sauce (see page 62)
grated cheese to sprinkle

Parboil zucchini in salted water for 6 to 8 minutes; leave to cool. Cut zucchini lengthwise and scoop out pulp; chop pulp and set aside. In a skillet, saute the garlic, onions, and beef in butter; add $^3/_4$ cup chopped zucchini pulp, parsley, oregano, salt and pepper, and wine; simmer for 25 minutes. Fill shells with beef and pulp mixture and place in baking pan, along with $^1/_2$ cup water. Top with bechamel sauce and grated cheese. Bake at 325° for 35 minutes or until slightly brown.

"The capon burns, the pig falls from the spit,
The clock hath strucken twelve."

Shakespeare

"That all-softening overpowering knell, the tocsin of the soul.
The dinner bell."

Lord Byron

"Other men live to eat, while I eat to live!"

Socrates

"If a recipe is once begun, never leave it till it's done, be the labor great or small, cook
it well or not at all."

George Gekas

Buy four or five partridges, three hares, sparrows to gobble greedily, some
goldfinches and parrots, chaffinches, and kestrels and anything else you can find."

Eubulus (3rd century B.C.)

POULTRY

Chicken Breasts with Avgolemono Sauce
(Kota me Avgolemono)

2 tablespoons butter

2 tablespoons oil

4 to 6 breasts, deboned

2 cups water

$^1/_2$ teaspoon salt

3 eggs

2 lemons, juice only

1 tablespoon flour or cornstarch

Combine butter and oil in skillet and heat. Add chicken and brown on each side for 10 minutes over medium heat. Add water and salt, bring to boil. Reduce heat and cover. Simmer for 30 minutes, or until tender.

Make avgolemono sauce: In a medium bowl, beat eggs until slightly foamy and light yellow. Add lemon juice and cornstarch; beat again. Stir a ladleful of pan juice slowly into avgolemono. Pour over chicken and remove from heat immediately. Serve over a bed of white rice. Makes 4 servings.

Wine Baked Chicken and Artichoke Hearts

The best thing about Greek cooking is it is usually prepared with simplicity—one or two steps and you are ready to bake the chicken.

1 3-pound chicken, quartered

2 cans (14 ounces) artichoke hearts, drained

1 can (15 ounces) tomato sauce

$^3/_4$ cup dry sherry or white wine

$^1/_4$ teaspoon oregano

1 teaspoon fresh basil or $^1/_4$ teaspoon dried garlic powder

salt and pepper

Remove skin from chicken. Place quartered chicken in baking pan. Arrange artichoke hearts around chicken pieces. Combine tomato sauce, wine, and spices, and season to taste with salt and pepper. Pour mixture over chicken. Bake for 45 minutes in 400° oven, basting occasionally. Serve with pilaf and a salad. Makes 4 to 5 servings.

Baked Chicken (Kotopoulo Psito)

Another savory chicken recipe for you to enjoy. Plaka Taverna in Manhattan bakes the chicken to perfection.

1 frying chicken (2$\frac{1}{2}$ pounds whole)
juice of 2 lemons
salt and pepper
1 teaspoon oregano

1 clove garlic, minced
4 tablespoons margarine or 2 tablespoons olive oil
2 tablespoons fresh tomato, peeled and chopped

Wash fryer in cooled water and pat dry. Rub chicken with juice of 1 lemon, salt, and pepper. Mix remaining lemon juice, oregano, garlic, and additional salt and pepper, and rub cavity of chicken. Place chicken in a pan with 1 cup water. In a small bowl, mix olive oil or margarine with chopped tomatoes; pour over chicken. Bake in a 450° oven until golden brown. Lower heat to 350° and bake uncovered for 30 minutes longer, basting and turning frequently. Serve with rice pilaf and yogurt. Makes 4 servings.

Athenian Chicken on the Grill

Greek cuisine becomes an outdoor affair—when the weather permits. Inclement weather usually prevails in New York, so prepare to bake the chicken in the oven. Sorry!

6 whole chicken breasts
$\frac{1}{2}$ cup Roditis wine
$\frac{1}{2}$ cup olive oil
$\frac{1}{4}$ cup freshly squeezed lemon juice
2 tablespoons dried oregano

1 teaspoon dried thyme
1 teaspoon dried basil
1 teaspoon salt
$\frac{1}{2}$ teaspoon pepper

Rinse chicken and pat dry. In a large bowl, combine wine, oil, lemon juice, herbs, salt, and pepper. Add chicken breasts, cover, and marinate overnight.

Cook on an outdoor grill, basting occasionally with remaining marinade. This can also be baked in a 350° oven for 1 hour, basting several times. Accompany with a Greek salad and a loaf of crusty bread. Opaa! Makes 6 servings.

Greek Chicken Oregano

The preparation of this dish couldn't be more simple. Double or triple the recipe for larger groups.

14 pieces of chicken (6 breasts and 8 thighs) with skin

salt and pepper

3 garlic cloves, peeled and split in half

juice of 2 large lemons

$1/2$ cup olive oil

3 to 4 tablespoons crumbled oregano

Rinse chicken under cold, running water. Pat dry with paper towels. Sprinkle lightly with salt and pepper to taste. Combine the remaining ingredients in a deep bowl. Place chicken pieces in the marinade and coat all pieces well. Cover tightly and refrigerate for 2 to 4 hours.

Drain all chicken pieces, reserving the marinade. Broil chicken pieces on both sides, basting continually with the remaining marinade until the chicken is tender. Rice pilaf is a must! Makes 6 to 8 servings.

NOTE: This chicken is also delicious cooked over charcoal. Turn and baste it often with remaining marinade until it is tender and crisp. Serve on a large platter garnished with chunks of lemon and sprigs of fresh mint.

Baked Chicken and Vegetables (Kota Tou Fournou)

Greek chicken dishes are exciting, easy, varied and have, in fact, provided for me a rich resource of recipes through the years.

1 medium onion, sliced thin	$^3/_4$ teaspoon dried basil
4 boneless chicken breasts, halved	2 cloves garlic, minced
Dijon mustard	$^1/_8$ teaspoon paprika
3 medium zucchini or yellow squash, sliced	salt and pepper
$^1/_2$ pound mushrooms, sliced	grated parmesan cheese
3 tablespoons butter	

Place sliced onion on bottom of 9 x 13 inch greased pan. Place chicken breasts over onion. Spread lightly with mustard. Season to taste with salt and pepper. Top with squash and mushrooms, and dot with butter. Sprinkle with basil, garlic, and paprika. Cover pan with foil. Bake in a 400° oven for 45 minutes. Remove foil and top with grated cheese. Complement with rice pilaf and a glass of white wine. Makes 4 servings.

Marinated Chicken Kebabs (Kotopoulo Souvlakia)

Frequent marination will reward your palate.

1 frying chicken, quartered	$^1/_4$ teaspoon pepper
$^1/_4$ cup butter	2 to 3 onions, quartered
$^1/_4$ cup olive oil	4 tomatoes, quartered
$^1/_2$ cup fresh lemon juice	4 to 5 (10-inch) skewers
1 tablespoon oregano	green pepper pieces (optional)

Remove skin from chicken and debone. Cut meat in $1^1/_2$-inch pieces. Melt butter in saucepan. Blend in oil, lemon juice, oregano, and pepper. Pour over chicken cubes. Marinate 4 to 5 hours at room temperature (less if temperature is above 80°). Separate onion pieces. Alternate chicken, onion pieces and tomatoes on skewers in that order. Cook over hot coals or under broiler, basting and turning frequently. Serve with rice pilaf and a glass of Roditis wine. Makes 4 servings.

Baked Chicken with Tomatoes (Kota me Domates)

The herbs may vary just a bit, but the tavernas in Astoria have been cooking this bird in a tapsie for decades. The tapsie is a large shallow pan, one of the handiest cooking utensils found in a Greek kitchen. No Greek bride would consider her dowry complete without one. Tapsie is also the baking pan, used for most sweet pastries—baklava and custard pie.

2 broiler chickens, disjointed	1 onion, thinly sliced
1 stick butter	1 tablespoon oregano
2 tablespoons oil	1 teaspoon marjoram
juice of 1 lemon	1 teaspoon savory
1 teaspoon salt	1 bay leaf
pepper	1/4 cup red wine (dry)
1 1/2 cans whole tomatoes (29 ounces)	

Wash chicken parts in cold water and pat dry. In a saute pan, heat butter and oil. Pour half of it into shallow baking pan and lay chicken pieces in it. Mix strained lemon juice in remaining mixture and baste chicken. Sprinkle with salt and pepper. Bake in a 350° oven for 30 to 35 minutes.

Place tomatoes and remaining ingredients in a pot. Bring to a boil and pour over chicken. Reduce oven heat to 325° and continue baking for 1 to 1 1/2 hours more. Serve with rice pilaf. Serves 4–6.

Lemon-Garlic Roast Chicken (Kotopoulo Lemonato)

Say "yes" to Manhattan tavernas' preparation of this bird.

1 roasting chicken, 2 1/2 pounds whole

1 whole lemon

2 cloves garlic, crushed

1/3 cup soy sauce (low sodium or regular)

3 tablespoons flour

1 can (10 3/4 ounces) condensed chicken broth

Heat oven to 350°. Rinse chicken and pat dry. Place chicken in roasting pan. Cut lemon in half and squeeze over chicken and in cavity. Add garlic to soy sauce and pour over chicken. Baste frequently during cooking. Bake until cooked through and juices run clear, about 1 hour.

Remove chicken from pan; keep warm on platter. Skim fat from pan juices. Whisk flour in pan juices over medium heat. Pour in chicken broth; cook and stir until smooth and thickened. Generally, this is served with rice and makes a fine meal. Frugal too! Makes 4 servings.

Chicken Sauteed with Tomato Sauce and Rice (Atzem Style)

In Epirus, a familiar method of cooking poultry is called atzem: combined with rice and served from the baking dish.

1 **frying chicken (2¹/₂ pounds), washed, dried, and cut into serving pieces**

5 **tablespoons butter**

1 **large onion, chopped**

salt and pepper

1 **stick cinnamon**

¹/₂ **cup tomato sauce**

1¹/₂ **cups long grain white rice**

In a cooking-serving casserole dish, heat butter and saute chicken with chopped onions, turning the chicken pieces constantly. Add salt and pepper to taste. Add cinnamon stick, tomato sauce, and just enough water to cover chicken. Bake in a 350° oven for 40 minutes. Remove from oven and check liquid to measure 3 cups; if necessary add water. Add rice and shake casserole a few times to mix the rice. Continue baking uncovered for 20 minutes longer, or until all the liquid is absorbed by the rice. Remove from oven and drape with a dry towel for 10 minutes. Serve hot. Yogurt and a green salad goes well with this dish. Makes 4 servings.

Chicken Stew (Kotopoulo Kapama)

If lamb is a Greek's best friend, what about chicken?

1 **chicken (2¹/₂ pounds), disjointed**

1 **lemon, juice only**

cinnamon

salt and pepper

3 **ounces butter**

3 **ounces olive oil**

6 **tomatoes, peeled and chopped**

2 **tablespoons tomato paste**

Wash chicken pieces in cold water and pat dry. In a bowl, add lemon juice, cinnamon, and salt and pepper to taste. Add chicken pieces and coat well with mixture.

In a large frying pan, heat butter and olive oil together, and brown chicken pieces on all sides. Remove chicken to platter and keep warm. Peel and chop tomatoes and add tomato paste and a cup of hot water to frying pan containing the butter and oil. Stir well and cook tomatoes until very soft. Return chicken to frying pan, coating chicken pieces in sauce on all sides. Cover and cook over low heat until chicken meat is soft and ready to fall off the bone. Petros says, "It's a very easy recipe to prepare." Makes 4 servings.

Marinated Fried Chicken (Kotopoulo Tiganito Marinate)

Hellenes like marinades, especially the Greeks of New York. They have the best concept of why Greek chicken dishes are so exciting.

1 frying chicken (2¹/₂ pounds) cut into serving pieces
salt and pepper
corn or peanut oil for frying
parsley (for garnish), chopped
flour (for coating)

Marinade for chicken:

¹/₄ cup olive oil   1 teaspoon oregano
¹/₄ cup lemon juice   1 bay leaf, crushed
¹/₂ cup white wine vinegar   2 peppercorns, crushed
¹/₄ cup white wine   4 coriander seeds, cracked
2 cloves garlic, sliced
¹/₂ onion, sliced thin

In a large bowl, combine all the ingredients for marinade and beat with a fork. Dip chicken in the marinade, coating the pieces on all sides. Cover and refrigerate for at least 2 hours. Drain, then season with salt and pepper to taste. In a paper bag add flour and chicken pieces. Shake lightly until chicken is coated with flour. Pour oil into a heavy skillet and heat until almost to the smoking point. Place the chicken in oil and fry to a light color on all sides. Remove chicken to a baking pan, and bake in a 350° oven for 50 minutes or until tender, pouring off oil as it collects in the pan. The chicken will be crisp and chestnut brown. Garnish with parsley. Serve with a tomato, cucumber salad, and crusty bread. Makes 4 servings.

Rice Stuffing for Any Fowl (Parayemisma me Rizi)

2 tablespoons butter

1$^1/_2$ cups rice

3 cups boiling water

$^1/_2$ teaspoon salt and pepper each

1 teaspoon basil

$^1/_8$ teaspoon thyme

$^1/_2$ pound feta cheese, crumbled

1 egg, beaten

$^1/_2$ cup raisins

2 tablespoons chopped almonds

Melt butter in saucepan. Add rice and stir for several minutes until rice is well coated. Add boiling water, salt, pepper, and herbs. Cover and simmer for 12 minutes. Set aside to slightly cool. Add feta cheese, egg, raisins, and chopped almonds. Stuff the fowl. Yields 6 cups.

Roast Stuffed Chicken #1 (Kotopoulo Yemisto)

Chicken is a superb Sunday dinner, one my mother used to prepare for economic reasons. This recipe gives one a complete dinner from one chicken.

1 whole broiler chicken, 3$^1/_2$ to 4 pounds

giblets

2 teaspoons salt

$^3/_4$ cup butter

2 heaped tablespoons pine nuts

$^1/_2$ cup rice

1 cup hot water

2 heaped tablespoons currants

$^1/_4$ teaspoon pepper

Rinse chicken and pat dry. Rub neck and body cavities lightly with salt.

Chop giblets into small pieces. In a small pan, melt $^1/_4$ cup butter. Add pine nuts and saute until pink. Remove pine nuts and saute giblets in same butter. Add rice; saute for 3 minutes. Add pine nuts, water, currants, salt, and pepper. Cover and cook slowly over medium heat for 10 minutes, or until the water is absorbed. Fill chicken about $^2/_3$ full with the stuffing, packing it loosely. Use skewer to close cavity. Using white cotton string, lace up like a boot and tie securely. Truss bird and roast.

Place chicken, breast side up, on a rack in a shallow roasting pan. Rub skin thoroughly with salad oil. If meat thermometer is used, insert in center of inside thigh muscle, without touching the bone. Roast in uncovered pan in a 375° oven for 1$^1/_2$ to 2 hours. Brush dry areas of skin occasionally with pan drippings. A large bowl of Greek salad and dry white wine will make a complete meal. Makes 4 to 6 servings.

Roast Stuffed Chicken #2 (Kotopoulo Yemisto)

Here is another easy-to-prepare dish. A superb dish for family or guests. This stuffing of pine nuts and herbs has a subtle blend of textures and flavors. The recipe comes from my dad.

1 roasting chicken (3 pounds), liver and heart reserved

salt, pepper, and nutmeg to taste

3 tablespoons butter

1 medium onion, minced

3 tablespoons chopped celery

3 tablespoons chopped parsley

2 tablespoons chopped dill

toast crumbs ($^{1}/_{2}$ cup)

$^{1}/_{2}$ cup milk, or more

2 tablespoons pine nuts

4 tablespoons melted butter

parsley (for garnish)

Wash chicken inside and out with cold water, dry, then sprinkle inside and out with salt and pepper and grate some nutmeg into the cavity. Set aside while preparing the stuffing.

Saute the chicken liver and heart in $^{1}/_{2}$ teaspoon of the butter. Chop liver and heart; set aside. Heat the remaining butter in a frying pan and cook onion until transparent. Add celery and saute for a few minutes. Add the parsley, dill, and stir in the toasted crumbs. Remove from heat; stir in milk and season with salt, pepper, and nutmeg (if necessary use more milk). Return to heat until the mixture boils. Add pine nuts and chopped liver stirring all the while.

Stuff the body cavity and close it tight with 3 to 4 skewers. Brush with melted butter and place, breast side down, in a baking dish. Bake in a 350° oven for 1$^{1}/_{2}$ hours, turning the chicken over every 30 minutes, brushing often with drippings. Place chicken on warm platter and garnish with parsley. Makes 4 servings.

Pan Fried Chicken Breast with Capers

Picatta means "sharp" in Italian. But to my niece and nephew, Canella and Mark Woyar, authors of this delightful chicken recipe, it meant making adjustments for a period of time to bring to my palate a flavor that I couldn't resist.
Preparation time 1 hour.

6 chicken breasts, remove the skin and debone

1 bunch green onions, chopped

1 large yellow onion, chopped fine

2 cloves garlic, crushed

4 tablespoons olive oil

1/2 cup flour

salt and pepper to taste

3 tablespoons butter

2 tablespoons dry sherry

2 tablespoons fresh lemon

1 tablespoon capers, chopped

3 tablespoons chicken stock

6 thin lemon slices

chopped parsley

Saute the yellow onion, garlic, and green onions in olive oil until tender. Remove from frying pan and set aside.

Pound chicken breast flat with a meat pounder. Mix the flour and salt and pepper together, and place on a large platter. Dip the chicken breast into the flour mixture. Lightly brown chicken breast in butter, 3 minutes on each side. Add sauteed onions and garlic. Over high heat add sherry, lemon juice, and capers. Add chicken stock and continue for a minute or so over high heat. Make sure that chicken gravy is evenly spread over chicken breast, before placing on serving platter.

Garnish with thin slices of lemon and the chopped parsley. A dry white wine will help the celebration.

Athenian-Style Roasted Chicken (Kota Psiti)

The wonderful thing about Greek cooking is that it is rarely complex. You can roast chicken along with Greek-style potatoes.

1- to 3-pound chicken, quartered or halved
$1/2$ lemon
2 teaspoons oregano
salt and pepper to taste
4 potatoes, peeled and quartered lengthwise

$1/3$ cup oil
$1/3$ cup lemon juice
1 teaspoon chopped lemon zest

Preheat oven to 375°. Rinse the chicken well in cold water and pat dry with paper towels. Place in a 9 x 12 inch roasting pan. Rub well with the lemon, and season with $1/2$ teaspoon oregano, and salt and pepper.

Add the potatoes around the chicken pieces and sprinkle with remaining oregano, and salt and pepper.

Combine oil, lemon juice, and lemon zest in small jar, shake to mix well. Pour over chicken and potatoes, coating well.

Roast uncovered until golden brown and tender, about 1½ hours, basting occasionally. Makes 3 servings.

Roast Stuffed Turkey (Ghallos Yemistos)

The traditional Greek stuffing for poultry includes chestnuts, which are plentiful in Greece.

8- to 10-pound turkey

salt and pepper

1 medium onion, chopped

1 cup butter

1 pound veal, minced

turkey livers, chopped

1 cup rice

1 cup hot water

$^1/_2$ cup currants or raisins

$^1/_2$ cup pine nuts, broken walnuts, or shredded almonds

1 pound chestnuts, boiled, peeled, and halved

Clean the turkey and wash thoroughly. Rub insides well with salt and pepper. Prepare the stuffing: Saute onion in a little butter until soft, then add the minced veal, turkey livers, salt and pepper, and cook stirring for a few minutes. Add rice, hot water and cook covered over a low heat for 10 minutes. Add currants, pine nuts, and chestnuts. Stuff turkey and sew up. Place breasts up on a rack in a roasting pan with $^1/_2$ cup hot water. Pour over turkey $^1/_4$ cup butter. Bake uncovered in a slow oven 325° for 4 to 5 hours. Baste frequently with remaining butter. Or, bake the turkey covered with foil, removing foil towards the end of cooking period.

"Wild vegetables fit to boil are the beet, mallow, sorrel, nettle, orach, iris bulbs, truffles, and mushrooms."

Diocles of Carystus in Health, Book 1

"I will cook for my love a banquet of beets and cabbages,
Leeks, potatoes, turnips, all such fruits ...
For my clever love, who has returned from farther than the far east;
We will laugh like spring above the steaming, stolid winter roots."

"Thanksgiving Dinner," Collected Poems
Edna St. Vincent Millay

"The best sauce for food is hunger and the best flavoring for drink, thirst."

Socrates

VEGETABLES

Fried Cauliflower (Kounopithi Tighanito)

1 medium-sized cauliflower

salted water

Fritter batter:

  1 cup flour

  2 eggs, beaten

  1/2 cup milk

  2 tablespoons melted butter

  salt and pepper to taste

  olive oil (for frying)

Separate fresh cauliflower and cut stems from flowerets. Cook in boiling salted water until tender, but firm. Drain well, cool, and dry with paper towels. Set aside.

In a bowl combine flour, beaten eggs, milk, melted butter, and salt and pepper to make batter. Dip flowerets into batter. Fry a few at a time in hot olive oil. Serve hot. Makes 4 servings.

Potato Patties (Patatokeftethes)

My cousin Nick, who is a cook at the Fast Food Tunnel Restaurant in Athens, knew that I was writing a cookbook and took the time to send me several recipes. Thanks, Nick.

2 pounds cooked mashed potatoes

2 eggs

1 cup grated parmesan cheese

2 tablespoons chopped parsley

salt and pepper to taste

1 small onion, chopped fine

flour

olive oil

Mix all ingredients except flour and olive oil. If mixture is too soft, add a little flour. Shape into balls the size of an egg. Roll in flour, flatten slightly, and arrange on a floured dish. Cover with wax paper and chill well. Fry patties in olive oil over medium heat until golden brown on both sides. Serve plain, with yogurt, or garlic sauce (see page 66). Makes 4 servings.

Baked Summer Vegetables (Briami)

Another example of what Greeks can do with some vegetables and olive oil. No meat, but what a feast!

1 pound zucchini (green squash)	1 1/2 cups olive oil
1 pound eggplant	1 cup hot water
1 pound potatoes, peeled	salt and pepper to taste
2 onions, chopped	parsley, chopped
1 1/2 pounds tomatoes	

Scrub and wash zucchini. Slice all vegetables in 1/2-inch pieces. Arrange in 10 x 13 inch baking pan. Add olive oil and one cup hot water. Sprinkle with salt, pepper, and parsley. Cover and bake in 325° oven for 1 1/2 hours, uncovering for the last 30 minutes. Makes 4 to 5 servings.

Corn on the Cob (Aravositos Kalamboki)

The French think that fresh corn is fit only for fodder. Street vendors in Athens sell this delicious vegetable hot from their portable braziers. Big business!

allow 2 cobs per person

butter

salt to taste

Place corn covered with husks in water for 5 minutes. Remove from water and peel. Place corn over charcoal brazier for 10 minutes, turning frequently. Brush with melted butter and salt. I'll bet you won't leave a kernel on the cob.

String Beans with Olive Oil (Fasolakia me Lathi)

2 1/2 pounds string beans	1 pound tomatoes, chopped
1 cup olive oil	3 tablespoons parsley, chopped
2 onions, sliced thin	salt and pepper to taste
1 clove garlic (optional)	1 heaped teaspoon sugar

Remove ends of string beans and wash in cold water. Cut string beans lengthwise into thin strips.

Heat the oil in a saucepan. Add onions and garlic; cook until soft. Add tomatoes, beans, parsley, salt and pepper, and sugar. Cover and cook over moderate heat for 1/2 hour, or until beans are tender. Serve cold. Makes 4 to 5 servings.

Boiled Summer Squash
(Vrasta Kolokithakia)

Although Greek chefs in New York may vary this simple recipe, they all agree on one thing: Don't cook it to death.

1 pound summer squash, preferably zucchini	juice of 1 lemon (or 2 tablespoons vinegar)
1 cup water	1/4 teaspoon salt
1/4 teaspoon sugar	dash white pepper
salt to taste	1/4 teaspoon oregano
1/2 cup olive oil	

Wash zucchini well, cut off ends of zucchini. Slice into 1-inch rounds. Place zucchini in a pan, add water, salt, and sugar. Cover and boil until soft, 12 to 15 minutes.

Mix all remaining ingredients well with a fork just before ready to serve. Pour over zucchini and serve. This sauce may be used with any hot or cold vegetable. Makes 4 servings.

Potatoes Stewed with Lemon
(Patates Lemonates)

2 1/2 pounds potatoes, peeled and quartered	juice of 1 lemon
1 teaspoon salt	2 cloves garlic, sliced thin
1/4 teaspoon pepper	chopped parsley
1 bay leaf	1/2 cup butter
2 cups hot water or beef stock	

In a large frying pan, combine all ingredients except parsley. Cover and cook on slow heat for 30 minutes or until potatoes are tender. Sprinkle with parsley. This potato dish will complement a menu of broiled chops, either pork or lamb. And by all means, make sure you broil those chops a la Greek style! Makes 4 servings.

Stewed Potatoes (Patates Yiahini)

3 pounds potatoes

2 medium-sized onions,
thinly sliced

1 cup olive oil

1–1 1/2 pounds ripe tomatoes,
peeled and sliced

salt and pepper to taste

parsley

2 cups hot water

Peel and wash potatoes. Cut into 1/3-inch slices and set aside in water.

Saute onions with oil in saucepan until soft. Add tomatoes and potatoes in layers. Sprinkle with salt, pepper, and parsley. Add 2 cups hot water, cover, and cook over a low heat for 30 minutes, or until potatoes are soft and sauce is thick.

For stewed potatoes with garlic (Patates plaki), substitute 3 to 4 cloves of sliced garlic for the onions. Makes 6 servings.

Okra with Tomatoes (Bamies me Domates)

1 pound small, fresh okra

1/2 cup vinegar

salt

3/4 cup olive oil

2 medium onions, peeled
and coarsely chopped

1 pound fresh or canned tomatoes,
peeled and chopped

salt and pepper to taste

parsley

1 teaspoon sugar

Trim the cone-shaped tops from the okra. Wash, drain, and place okra in a bowl. Sprinkle with salt and vinegar and set aside for half an hour (this prevents okra from splitting while cooking). Wash okra again and dry thoroughly.

Heat the olive oil in large frying pan and add the chopped onions. Cook gently until the onion is tender. Add the okra and cook, tossing lightly until slightly browned. Add tomatoes (if fresh), salt and pepper, and sugar. Cover and simmer gently for 45 minutes, or until tender. Makes 4 servings.

Vegetable Stew with Olive Oil (Lahanika Thiafora me Lathi)

An enjoyable, tasty stew that is served cold.

1 pound green beans	2 medium onions, sliced thin
1 pound eggplant	2 tablespoons salt
1 pound zucchini	$1/2$ teaspoon pepper
2 large green peppers	2 teaspoons sugar
1 pound potatoes	$1 1/4$ cups olive oil
$1 1/2$ pounds tomatoes	chopped parsley

Wash green beans in cold water. Remove ends and cut into 2-inch pieces. Wash and cut eggplant into small pieces. Scrub zucchini, cut off ends, and rinse. Cut in halves lengthwise and crosswise into 1-inch pieces. Wash and remove seeds from peppers and cut into strips. Peel, wash, and cut potatoes into bite-size pieces. Wash, peel, and cut tomatoes into slices. Peel, wash, and slice onions. Layer vegetables in a 9 x 13 inch baking dish. Add salt, pepper, sugar and olive oil. Sprinkle with parsley. Bake covered in preheated 325° oven $1 1/2$ hours, until vegetables are soft and most of the liquid has evaporated. Serve cold. Makes 6 to 8 servings.

Green Beans Braised with Mint and Potatoes
(Fasolakia me Patates)

The vegetable cuisine of Greece is extraordinarily natural and versatile. It ranges from the simple preparation of lowly greens, bathed in just olive oil, to dishes like this one.

3 tablespoons olive oil and butter, mixed

1 cup tomato sauce

1 pound fresh green beans, trimmed and cut

1 tablespoon chopped fresh parsley

2 medium potatoes, peeled and cut in sixths lengthwise

salt and pepper

$1 1/2$ teaspoons fresh mint, chopped

Heat the olive oil and butter in an enameled pan and mix in the tomato sauce. Add green beans, parsley, and enough water to almost cover. Tuck potato slices in between green beans. Partially cover pan and simmer for 30 minutes. Add chopped mint, and season with salt and pepper to taste. Stir with a wooden spoon. Cook uncovered until beans and potatoes are fork-tender. Serve vegetables in a warm bowl. Goes well with chops or fish, or serve as a main course, along with crusty bread. Serves 4.

Green Beans with Tomatoes (Fasolakia Prasina Yiahni)

When one tastes a vegetable or fruit picked fresh, he/she is forever haunted by the purity of the flavor. After savoring the home-grown vegetables of Greece, many Americans will never again be satisfied by our commercially grown produce.

1 **pound string beans**

1/4 **cup olive oil**

3 **teaspoons butter**

2 **onions, chopped fine**

1 **clove garlic, chopped**

1 **pound tomatoes, chopped**

1 **cup water**

1 **teaspoon thyme**

1 **teaspoon dried mint**

salt and pepper

1/2 **pound mushrooms (optional)**

Wash string beans in cold water, drain, and set aside. Heat oil and butter in sauce pan. Add onions and garlic and saute until onions are soft. Add tomatoes, and boil uncovered to evaporate most of the liquid, about 10 minutes. Add cup of water, thyme, mint, and salt and pepper to taste; bring to boil. Stir in string beans, cover, and simmer until beans are tender. Add additional water if needed. Makes 4 servings.

NOTE: Artichokes, okra, green pepper, and frozen string beans can be substituted for fresh green beans. Lamb, veal, or beef chunks can be added for a delightful Greek stew.

Stuffed Red Tomatoes (Yemistes Domates)

Stella Pavlatos has given several excellent recipes to the Saint Nicholas Greek Orthodox Church cookbook (Our Kozina). It was early spring that Stella and I put on our tall chef's hats and made this stuffed tomato dish for a family affair. Big hit!

15 medium tomatoes	salt, pepper, and ground allspice
1 1/2 pounds ground beef	1/2 cup rice
2 large onions, chopped fine	2 cans (10 ounces) tomato sauce
1 stick margarine	1/2 cup vegetable oil
1 tablespoon Worcestershire sauce	sugar to taste

Carefully cut tops of tomatoes and reserve. Scoop out pulp of tomatoes, chop, and set aside. Place tomato shells in a baking dish. Sprinkle sugar lightly inside of tomato shells. In a skillet, saute onions in margarine. Add ground beef, Worcestershire sauce, and salt, pepper, and allspice to taste. Add tomato pulp to meat mixture. Continue cooking until tomato is soft. Add rice and mix thoroughly. Spoon mixture into tomato shells and cap tomatoes with tomato tops. Combine tomato sauce and vegetable oil, and pour over tomatoes. Bake at 350° for 1 hour, basting occasionally. Serve with Greek cheeses, olives, sliced cucumbers, crusty bread, and Roditis wine. Makes 15 servings.

Stuffed Tomato with Feta Cheese (Domates me Feta)

It is important that you use the ripest tomatoes. If tomatoes aren't quite ripe, place them in a brown paper bag and keep in a dark place for a couple of days to ripen.

5 ripe medium tomatoes

3 tablespoons finely chopped scallions, use most of the green stem

3 tablespoons finely chopped parsley

3/4 cup feta cheese, crumbled

1/2 cup bread crumbs

4 tablespoons olive oil

Carefully cut tops off tomatoes. Using a spoon, carefully scoop out pulp and seeds. Save pulp and discard seeds. Coarsely chop the tomato pulp. Combine pulp, scallions, parsley, feta cheese, bread crumbs, and olive oil. Mix well. Spoon mixture into the hollowed-out tomatoes. Preheat oven to 350°. Place tomatoes right side up on baking sheet and bake for 15 to 20 minutes. Makes 5 servings.

Fried Artichoke Hearts with Egg and Lemon Sauce
(Tighanito Aginares me Avgolemono)

This dish is delicious as an appetizer or a side dish.
The avgolemono sauce is easy to prepare and can be used for other fried vegetables.

20-ounce package frozen artichoke hearts

2   eggs, well beaten

1   cup fine bread crumbs

1/4 cup grated kefalotiri or parmesan cheese

vegetable oil (for deep-frying)

salt and pepper

Dip artichoke hearts in egg, then in flour, then in egg again, and coat well with bread crumbs mixed with grated cheese.

Heat enough oil in a heavy frying pan to cover artichokes. When oil is hot enough to sizzle, add artichokes a few at a time. Cook, turning gently, until golden brown. Use a slotted spoon to remove artichokes. Drain on paper towel. Salt and pepper to taste. Makes 6 servings.

NOTE: See egg and lemon sauce recipe on page 64. This sauce can be used as a dip or drizzled over the tops of the artichokes.

Spinach Saute (Spanaki Saute)

Spinach is enjoyable in so many ways. This is one of the many excellent Greek recipes for spinach. Always use fresh ingredients when possible, and there is no substitute for butter.

2 1/2 pounds fresh spinach

1/2 cup butter

3   scallions, chopped fine

salt and pepper to taste

chopped fresh dill

Wash spinach thoroughly several times in cold water, and drain well. In a saucepan, heat butter and saute scallions for 5 minutes, or until soft. Add spinach, salt, pepper, and dill; stir and cover. Cook for 15 minutes, or until just tender. Makes 4 servings.

Spinach Souffle (Spanaki Souffle)

This souffle is so easy to prepare. For spinach lovers who prefer a low cholesterol spinach souffle, use egg beaters and low cholesterol cheese. I have prepared this recipe both ways. Believe me, you can't tell the difference.

20 ounces frozen chopped spinach
2 pounds small curd creamed cottage cheese
1/4 pound sharp cheddar cheese, grated
1/4 pound swiss cheese, grated
6 eggs, beaten
6 to 7 tablespoons flour
1/4 pound butter, melted
4 scallions, chopped and sauted

Allow spinach to stand at room temperature to defrost completely (do not soak in water). Squeeze very dry and combine with remaining ingredients, mixing well. Pour into greased 9 x 13 inch baking dish. Bake in preheated 350° oven for 1 hour, or until brown. Serve with a crisp tossed salad and crusty bread. Makes 6 servings.

Leeks Stewed with Tomatoes (Prassa me Domates)

Leeks are a mild and delightful member of the onion family that have been cultivated for centuries.

2 bunches leeks
1 cup chicken broth
1 (10-ounce) can of tomatoes
1 medium onion, chopped
1 stalk celery, chopped
few sprigs fresh parsley
pinch of thyme
vegetable oil
salt and pepper to taste
juice of 1 lemon

To clean leeks, cut off the roots and slice the leek in half lengthwise. Cut into pieces and remove outer pieces that are too tough to eat. As you go up into the greener part, remove the outer layers and use the inner pieces. Rinse well with cold water and drain. In an enameled pan, cook covered in broth for 5 to 8 minutes. Add tomatoes, onion, celery, parsley, thyme, oil, and salt and pepper. Simmer until tender, adding lemon juice at very end of cooking time. Makes 4 servings.

Baked Eggplant Slices

I enjoy the simplicity of this dish. Since it can be served cold or warm, it is versatile.

2 medium-sized eggplants
1 tablespoon salt
$^3/_4$ cup olive oil
juice of 1 lemon
$^1/_2$ teaspoon dried oregano
black pepper and salt to taste

With a fork, score the eggplant lengthwise, cut into slices $^1/_4$ inch thick and sprinkle with salt. Drain in a colander for 2 hours and then rinse with cold water and place on paper towels. Pat dry.

Pan brown the slices using $^1/_4$ cup olive oil. Remove when lightly brown and place on a baking sheet and bake in a pre-heated oven at 375°, until slices are very tender. Remove to a serving platter and allow to cool. Mix remaining olive oil, lemon juice, oregano, salt and pepper. Dress the slices with this sauce.

NOTE: This eggplant tastes very good with garlic sauce (skordalia) page 66.

Lima Beans with Greek Tomato Sauce

This recipe is served in most New York Greek restaurants. One bowl of these lima beans, along with some feta cheese and crusty bread—you have yourself a meal.

$^1/_2$ pound dried lima beans
5 tablespoons olive oil
3 cloves garlic, sliced thin
1 yellow onion, peeled and sliced thin
1 large ripe tomato, cut in bite size pieces
4 tablespoons tomato paste
1 cup Greek tomato sauce on page 66
$^1/_2$ cup dry red wine
salt and pepper to taste
$^1/_2$ cup parsley, chopped
$^1/_4$ teaspoon cinnamon (optional)

Soak beans in water overnight and drain. Add olive oil in a 4-quart casserole. Saute the onions and garlic until clear. Add tomato paste and tomato sauce and saute for 10 minutes.

Add all remaining ingredients, including the beans, cover, and simmer until the beans are tender (don't overcook), about 40 minutes.

Stuffed Tomatoes with Rice (Yemistes Domates me Rizi)

15 medium-sized tomatoes

1 teaspoon sugar

3 cups onions, chopped fine

1 1/2 cups olive oil

1/2 cup raisins or currants

1/2 cup fresh dill

1/2 cup parsley, chopped

1/2 cup pine nuts

1 cup rice

1/2 cup water, add more if necessary

salt and pepper to taste

Slice off tops of tomatoes. Scoop out pulp, chop and set aside. Place tomato shells in a large casserole. Sprinkle inside of tomato shells with salt and sugar. Saute onions in 1/4 cup olive oil until soft. Add dill, currants, parsley, pine nuts, rice, and chopped pulp. Add 1 cup olive oil and mix well. Saute for 5 minutes. Season to taste. Fill tomatoes with mixture. Cover with tomato tops and pour 1/4 cup olive oil with water over tomatoes.

In a 350° preheated oven, bake for 50 minutes or until rice is cooked, basting occasionally.

MACARONI
AND RICE

Greek Style Macaroni (Makaronada)

A classic dish, this can be served as a main course with a salad or as a side dish with chops.

1   pound macaroni
grated kefalotiri or parmesan cheese
1/4 pound butter

For every pound of macaroni, boil one gallon water. When water is boiling put in salt, according to taste, and add macaroni, stirring well. Cover pot and let come to a boil on high flame, for 10 to 20 minutes (cooking time varies, depending on the shape or cut of macaroni). Remove from flame and add one pint of cold water. Drain well. Sprinkle generously with grated cheese. Melt butter in a large skillet until it foams and turns golden brown, stirring so that it will not burn. Pour butter over macaroni and sprinkle again with grated cheese. Noodles or spaghetti can be substituted for macaroni. Makes 4 servings.

Baked Macaroni (Makaronia Sto Fournou)

1   pound macaroni
salt
1/2 cup butter
6   tablespoons flour

3 1/2 cups milk
1/4 teaspoon white pepper
1 1/2 cups grated kefalotiri
  and gruyere cheeses

Cook macaroni in 4 quarts of boiling salted water. Drain well and return to the pan. Add 1/4 cup melted butter and mix well. Add the remaining butter to a saucepan. Blend in flour. Add milk and salt and pepper, stirring continuously. Cook over low heat for 5 minutes.

Place half of macaroni in a greased casserole (youvetsi) dish. Distribute 1 cup of cheese over macaroni. Pour sauce over cheese. Sprinkle remaining cheese over top.

Bake, uncovered, in a 350° oven for 30 minutes. Serves 5 to 6.

NOTE: A milder cheese, such as parmesan, can be substituted in this recipe.

Spaghetti with Tomato Sauce (Spaghetti me Saltsa Domata)

2¹/2 pounds tomatoes,
  peeled and diced

¹/3 cup olive oil

2 cloves garlic, split

1¹/2 teaspoons salt

¹/4 teaspoon pepper

1 tablespoon sugar

parsley, chopped

1 pound spaghetti

salt

¹/2 cup butter

cheese, grated

In a saucepan add tomatoes, oil, garlic, 1¹/2 teaspoons salt, pepper, and sugar. Cook over low heat for about 1 hour. Add parsley.

Cook spaghetti in 4 quarts of salted water. Drain spaghetti well. In a small saucepan, heat butter until golden brown. Place spaghetti on a large serving platter, and pour butter over spaghetti. Cover spaghetti with sauce or serve sauce separately. Sprinkle with plenty of grated cheese. Makes 4 servings.

Spaghetti with Meat Sauce (Spaghetti me Kima)

This recipe gets an excellent rating in the Big Apple.

1 medium onion, chopped fine

2 cloves garlic, minced

2 tablespoons butter

1 pound ground beef

¹/8 teaspoon cloves, ground

¹/4 teaspoon cinnamon, ground

1 bay leaf

3 to 4 ounces tomato paste,
  diluted with equal part of water

¹/2 cup white wine

1 cup water

1 pound spaghetti

¹/4 pound butter

mizithra or parmesan cheese, grated

Saute onion and garlic in 2 tablespoons butter until onion is soft; add meat and brown well. Add cloves, cinnamon, bay leaf, and tomato paste, mixing well. Add wine and water; lower flame and simmer for ³/4 of an hour. Meanwhile, cook spaghetti in boiling salted water until tender, and drain well.

In a skillet, melt ¹/4 pound butter over spaghetti, and with two serving forks, mix lightly. Spoon meat sauce over spaghetti, and sprinkle generously with grated cheese. Serve remaining meat sauce in a side bowl along with an additional bowl of grated cheese. Consider this a meal, when served with a green salad and a glass of wine. Makes 6 servings.

Baked Macaroni or Spaghetti with Meat (Youvetsi)

Macaroni is a general term for all pasta in Greece. Only spaghetti keeps its own name. Treat yourself to Greek wine for a complete meal.

2 pounds lamb (cut in 5 portions)	1 tablespoon tomato paste
1/2 cup butter	salt and pepper to taste
1 medium onion, minced	1 pound macaroni or spaghetti
1 clove garlic, minced	grated kefalotiri or parmesan cheese
2 cups tomato juice	

Heat butter in saucepan and brown meat on all sides. Add onion and garlic, and saute until onion is soft. Add tomato juice, tomato paste, salt, pepper, and enough hot water to cover the meat. Cover and simmer over a low heat until meat is tender and sauce is thick.

Boil macaroni or spaghetti in boiling salted water. Drain. Put half the macaroni into a buttered baking dish and cover with meat mixture. Add remaining macaroni over meat and spread tomato sauce on top. Sprinkle with grated cheese and bake in a 350° oven for 15 to 20 minutes. I prefer to serve with plenty of kefalotiri cheese on the side. Makes 5 servings.

Square Noodles with Meat Sauce (Hilopittes Kapama)

This very basic dish, found on the menu at most tavernas in Manhattan, makes a wonderful side dish. At home, serve with a tossed salad for a frugal meal.

1 pound ground beef

1 tablespoon butter

1 can (6 ounces) tomato paste
diluted with 3 ounces water

2 teaspoons allspice

dash of nutmeg and cinnamon

salt and pepper to taste

1 pound square noodles, cooked and drained

grated cheese

Saute meat in butter until brown. Stir in tomato paste, spices, salt, and pepper. Cook covered over low heat for 10 minutes, stirring frequently. While sauce cooks, boil noodles in salted water until done and drain. Pour sauce over noodles. Sprinkle with grated cheese and serve. Makes 4 servings.

Steamed White Rice

To more than half of the world's population, rice is the basic life-sustaining food, supplying more than 80 percent of daily food-energy requirement. Rice was originally cultivated in Southeast Asia about 3,000 years B.C., and from there it spread all over the world, to be embraced by different cultures.

2 1/2 cups water	1 tablespoon butter
1 cup rice	1 teaspoon salt

Bring 2 1/2 cups water to a boil. Stir in 1 cup rice, 1 teaspoon salt and, if desired, 1 tablespoon butter. Cover tightly and simmer 20 minutes. Remove from heat. Let stand covered until water is absorbed, about 5 minutes.

For softer rice, use more water and simmer longer. For firmer rice use less water and simmer for a shorter time. One cup of uncooked rice makes 3 cups cooked rice.

Cooked rice can be frozen for convenience. To do so, cook the rice ever-so-slightly less than normal. Drain rice and rinse under cold water until cooled. This step effectively stops the cooking process. Spread rice on paper towels and blot out excess moisture. Portion in airtight plastic bags and freeze. Rice will keep for several months.

To thaw frozen rice quickly, use the microwave oven. Place rice on a paper plate and heat on high power in one minute increments. After each minute, work through the bag to separate the grains of rice as they thaw. Rice can also be thawed at room temperature or overnight in the refrigerator.

Baked Rice (Pilafi Sto Fournou)

Greeks and Italians eat more rice than any other European nations. The Greeks roll it in grape leaves, and the Italians prepare creamy risotto, but rice generally is seen as a side dish.

3 to 4 tablespoons butter

1 1/2 cups raw long-grain white rice

salt and white pepper

3 1/2 cups hot chicken stock

In a saucepan, heat butter over medium heat. Add rice and saute until transparent, stirring constantly. Be careful not to brown.

Transfer to a buttered baking dish and add salt and pepper to taste. Add hot chicken stock and stir. Bake, covered, in a preheated 350° oven for 40 minutes, or until the rice is tender and all liquid has been absorbed. Remove from oven, uncover, and drape with a dry towel for 10 minutes. Serve warm. Makes 4 servings.

Rice Pilaf (Ryzi Pilafi)

I stole this recipe from Helen, my wife. She's the one who taught me what good pilaf is all about.

1/4 pound butter
2/3 cups onion, finely chopped
2 cups rice
4 1/4 cups boiling chicken broth or bouillion
1 teaspoon salt
pinch of white pepper

In a saucepan over low heat, heat butter. Add onion and cook until onion is transparent. Add rice and stir until all the grains are evenly coated. Cook 3 to 4 minutes, but do not brown. Add salt and pepper. Pour in broth and stir. Cover and simmer for 25 minutes or until rice is tender and liquid is absorbed. Let rice stand, covered, for 10 minutes before serving. Serve with meat, chicken or with a sauce. Makes 6 servings.

Wheat Pilaf

Food of the ancients tastes fresh and flavorful, such as sea bass marinated in olive oil, vinegar, and fresh herbs, served with wheat pilaf.

5 tablespoons olive oil, divided
1 cup bulgur (cracked wheat)
2 1/2 cups water
3 tablespoons pine nuts
1/2 cup red cabbage, cut into thin strips
3 tablespoons Zante currants
1 teaspoon ground coriander
2 tablespoons finely chopped fresh spearmint
1 teaspoon cumin
salt and pepper

In a small skillet, heat 2 tablespoons olive oil. Add bulgur and cook, stirring continuously until bulgur is golden. Be careful not to burn.

In a 2-quart saucepan, bring 2 1/2 cups of water to boil. Add bulgur; reduce heat and simmer, covered, for 20 to 25 minutes, until water is absorbed.

In a small skillet, cook pine nuts in 1 tablespoon olive oil over medium heat until lightly browned. Set aside.

Heat remaining 2 tablespoons of oil in small skillet. Saute cabbage until tender.

Place cooked bulgur in large bowl. Add pine nuts, cabbage, currants, coriander, spearmint, and cumin. Season with salt and pepper to taste. Taste and adjust seasoning if necessary. Serve hot. Serves 6 to 8 as a side dish.

Pilaf with Tomato Sauce (Pilafi me Saltsa Domata)

New York restaurants claim the copyrights to many lamb and chicken favorites. This version of rice pilaf is simply delicious.

1 medium onion, chopped fine	1 tablespoon celery, chopped
3/4 cup butter	1 tablespoon parsley, chopped
2 cloves garlic, chopped fine	salt and pepper
1 1/2 pounds ripe tomatoes, peeled and strained	3 cups rice

Saute onion in half the butter until golden. Add garlic and cook until soft. Add tomatoes, celery, parsley, and salt and pepper; simmer for 30 minutes. Pass sauce through a strainer, or puree in a blender, and return to the pot. Cook over low flame until thick. Prepare the rice as directed in steamed rice (see page 141). Brown the remaining butter and pour it over the rice, mixing lightly. Pack rice into a mold, then turn it out onto a serving platter. Pour tomato sauce over the rice. Makes 8 to 10 servings.

Spinach with Rice (Spanakoryso)

In New York, every Greek restaurant has a spinach and rice dish that you won't believe! The secret is fresh spinach and tomatoes. An easy dish to prepare. Frugal too!

1 pound fresh spinach	1/2 teaspoon oregano
1/2 cup olive oil	1/2 cup rice
1/2 stick butter	1 cup water
1 onion, chopped fine	1 cup fresh tomatoes, chopped
1 tablespoon dried dill	salt and pepper to taste

Remove and discard coarse stems of spinach. Wash leaves well and sprinkle lightly with salt. Stir to spread salt evenly. After 20 minutes, rinse off salt and squeeze out excess water. Cut up spinach.

In a heavy pot, heat olive oil and butter and saute onions until soft. Add dill and oregano. Stir well. Add rice and stir until grains are well coated. Add water, salt, and pepper and cook for 10 minutes. Add spinach and tomatoes; cook till rice is tender. Accompany with feta cheese and crusty bread. I have enjoyed this spinach dish as a main dish many times. Makes 4 servings.

"A loaf of bread, the Walrus said,
Is what we chiefly need;
Pepper and vinegar besides
Are very good indeed."

Lewis Carroll

"They that have no other meat,
Bread and butter are glad to eat."

Thomas Fuller

"Here is bread, which strengthens man's heart, and therefore called the staff
of life."

Matthew Henry

"A sweet, some myrtle-berries, a cheese-cake, almonds."

Deipnosophistae, 200 AD.

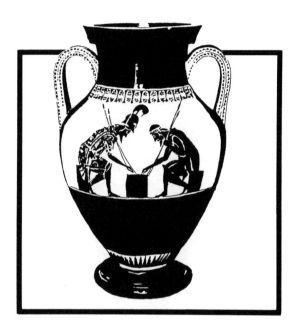

BREADS &
SWEETS

Greek Bread

Bread is extremely popular in Greece. It is found on the Greek table at all meals. In fact, lunch consists of fresh bread, cheese, and olives.

1 package yeast
1/3 cup warm water
1 cup milk
1/4 cup shortening
2 tablespoons sugar
1 teaspoon salt
3 to 4 cups flour

Soften yeast in a small amount of water. In a saucepan, combine milk, shortening, sugar, and salt. Heat. Stir until sugar and shortening are dissolved. Cool until mixture is lukewarm. Pour mixture into bowl. Stir in 1 cup flour; beat well. Add yeast; beat until smooth. Gradually mix in remaining flour to make moderately stiff dough. Place dough on floured surface; knead until smooth and satiny. Place dough in a greased bowl, cover, and allow to rise in a warm place until dough will retain the impression of a finger. Punch gas from dough and shape into two loaves. Place in greased bread pans and allow to rise until double in size. Bake in an oven at 375° for 45 minutes or until done.

Wheat Bread (Psomi Sitarenio)

2 packages yeast
4 cups lukewarm water
1/2 cup salad oil
2 teaspoons salt
3 tablespoons sugar
3 cups white flour
8 cups whole wheat flour

In a large bowl, dissolve yeast in lukewarm water. Add oil, salt, sugar, and white flour. Mix well. Stir in enough whole wheat flour to make a soft dough. Knead until mixture is smooth and elastic. Place dough in a greased bowl, cover, and allow to rise in a warm place until dough will retain impression of a finger. Punch gas from dough and shape into three loaves. Place in greased bread pans and cover and allow to rise until double in size (about 30 minutes). Bake in 350° oven for about 45 minutes. Remove from pan immediately. Place on rack to cool. Makes 3 loaves.

Holiday Bread (Tsoureki)

Tsoureki is bread that mothers make on religious festivals, Sundays, and holidays. For New Year's Day, it is called vasilopita, and is baked with money inside. It's called christopsomo on Christmas and decorated with a cross; on Easter, lambropsomo, and topped with dyed red eggs.

2 tablespoons dry or cake yeast	7 cups all-purpose flour, unsifted
1/4 cup warm water	1/2 cup sugar
1/2 teaspoon each:	1/2 teaspoon salt
cinnamon,	1/2 cup milk
anise seeds,	1/4 pound butter or 6 tablespoons oil
orange peel	3 eggs
1 bay leaf	Topping:
1/4 teaspoon mahaleb (optional)	egg yolk
4 grains mastic or 1 ounce ouzo (optional)	1/4 cup sesame seeds
1/2 cup water	

Dissolve yeast in warm water and set aside. In a saucepan, combine cinnamon, anise seeds, orange peel, bay leaf, mahaleb, and mastic with 1/2 cup water and bring to a boil. Set aside to steep and cool. Put flour, sugar, and salt in a large bowl. Heat milk; remove from fire, add butter or oil, and allow to cool slightly.

Make a hole in the middle of flour mixture and mix in eggs, yeast, milk, and flavored water, after removing the bay leaf. Use spoon or paddle to push flour from sides into center and mix. Knead dough on lightly floured board until smooth, about 20 to 25 minutes. Place in an oiled bowl. Cover with towel dampened with hot water and set in warm, draft-free place until bulk has doubled, about 4 to 6 hours.

When doubled in size, punch down and knead for 5 to 7 minutes. Pinch off two pieces of dough, each the size of a small apple. To make byzantine cross roll each ball of dough into long rope, 12 to 16 inches long. Slit the ends down 5 inches. Coil each slit in opposite directions. Form a cross with the ropes on top of loaf which meets at the exact center. Do not press flat. Glaze cross with egg yolk. Set aside to rise once again, about 2 hours. **Do not cover with towel.** Bake in 350° oven for 1 hour.

Easter Bread (Tsoureki)

Follow directions for Holiday bread, adding an extra ¹/₂ cup sugar. Place a hard-boiled egg dyed red in the center of the loaf before the second rising. Glaze with egg yolk and sprinkle with sesame seeds. Bake as above.

New Year's Day Bread (Vasilopita)

Follow directions for Holiday bread, adding an extra ¹/₂ cup sugar. Wrap coins of any denomination in aluminum foil and put into dough when kneading it. Shape in a large round loaf. Decorate with walnuts, cherries, or almonds. Set aside to rise in a warm place. Bake as above. The belief is that he who finds the coin will have good luck the coming year.

Sour Cherry Preserve (Visino Glyko)

This is the traditional Greek welcome for a visitor—spoon of sweets.

2¹/₂ pounds sour cherries

2¹/₂ pounds sugar

2   cups water

juice of 1 large lemon

Wash the cherries and remove the pits, being careful to keep them whole. Put into saucepan in layers with the sugar. Add water and boil for 25 minutes, stirring often and removing the froth. Leave overnight in the syrup. The following day add the lemon juice and boil until syrup is thick.

Test the syrup by dropping a little onto a saucer. If the drops do not spread, setting point is reached. Spoon into sterilized jars. Screw on lids. Store in a cool dry place. Yields 1¹/₂ pints.

Cherry Preserve (Kerasi Glyko)

Prepare as for Sour Cherry Preserve, except decrease sugar to 2 pounds and water to 1¹/₂ cups. Yields 1¹/₂ pints.

NOTE: You must sterilize jars first. Place them in a large pot, cover with hot water and bring to a boil for a few minutes.

Spoon Halvah

2 cups sugar

5 cups water

1 1/2 cups olive oil

3 cups farina

1/2 cup pignolia nuts

cinnamon

Boil sugar and water to make syrup. Heat oil in saucepan. When oil begins to boil, reduce heat and stir in farina; stirring constantly until the mixture is golden brown. Add pignolia nuts and syrup; blend until smooth. Cool mixture for 30 minutes. Using a tablespoon, spoon portions onto a serving dish. Sprinkle with cinnamon. Makes 12 servings.

Farina Diamonds (Halva)

1 quart milk

1/4 pound butter

1 1/2 cups sugar

1 cup farina

cinnamon

walnut halves

Boil milk, add sugar, and cook 10 minutes. In a heavy saucepan, heat butter. Add farina, stirring constantly until farina is golden brown. Add milk slowly, stirring until mixture thickens. Pour mixture into 9-inch greased pan and sprinkle with cinnamon. Cool and cut in diamond-shaped pieces, centering a walnut half on each piece. Makes 10 servings.

Grape Spoon Sweet (Staphylia Glyko)

My cousin, Demitra Pappas, who is the pastry cook at the Taverna Sigalas, located in Monastiraki Square, sent me this recipe for my cookbook. Thanks cousin!

2   **pounds seedless white grapes**
3   **cups sugar**
1   **cup water**
1   **cinnamon stick**
1   **tablespoon lemon juice**
$^1/_2$ **cup almonds, blanched and slivered**

Wash grapes in cold water. In a large saucepan, combine grapes, sugar, water, and cinnamon stick. Bring to a boil and skim froth. Cook over medium heat, stirring occasionally, until syrup thickens, about 45 minutes. Remove from heat.

When mixture has cooled slightly, remove cinnamon stick. Stir in lemon juice and almonds. Spoon into sterilized half-pint jars. Make sure the lids are on tight. Store in a cool place. Makes 3 pints.

Almond Pears (Amygthalota)

This sweet recipe comes from the island of Hydra. It's an original.

1   **pound blanched almonds**
1   **cup sugar**
5   **tablespoons fine semolina (cream of wheat)**
confectioners' sugar
$1^1/_2$ **cups orange flower water**
butter
cloves
flour

Grind almonds fine and mix well with 2 tablespoons sugar. Add remaining sugar, semolina, and 6 tablespoons orange flower water. Knead mixture to form a soft dough. If too stiff add 1 or 2 tablespoons orange flower water. Using your hands, shape the dough into pears. At the end of each pear, insert 1 clove for stalk. Arrange on a buttered and floured baking sheet. Bake in a 350° oven for 20 minutes. Remove almond pears from oven to cool. Dip pears into orange flower water and coat with confectioners' sugar. Wait 1 minute and coat them again in confectioners' sugar. Makes 24 pears.

Yogurt (Yiaourti)

This is a classic dessert in all of Greece. With the popularity of yogurt in our country, and the many ways of serving it, why not make your own? Try a drizzle of honey over yogurt.

1 quart milk

¹/₂ cup cream

2 tablespoons yogurt

Bring milk and cream to a boil and simmer for 2 minutes, stirring constantly. Pour in earthware bowl and let cool to 115°.
Dilute the yogurt into a few tablespoons of warm milk and add to the rest of the milk. Blend well. Cover the bowl; wrap snugly in a towel or blanket and allow to stand in a warm place overnight. When yogurt is set, store in refrigerator. Makes 1 quart.

Fresh Fruit and Yogurt (Frouta Ke Yiaourti)

Although most Greeks end their meal with a simple dessert of cold fresh fruit, you may want to top off your Greek feasts with this easy to prepare dessert.

4 cups cut-up mixed fresh fruit (such as various melons, apples, grapes, peaches, orange segments and assorted berries)

¹/₄ cup slivered almonds

1 cup (8 ounces) plain, lowfat yogurt

3 tablespoons honey

1¹/₂ tablespoons grated lemon rind

In a medium mixing bowl, combine yogurt, honey, and lemon rind. Place fruit and almonds in serving bowl. Stir gently to combine. Pour yogurt mixture over fruit and serve as a buffet or individual dessert bowls. Makes 5 to 6 servings.

Deep Fried Honey Doughnuts (Loo-koo-mah-thes)

Would you believe I got this delicious doughnut recipe at a "taste of ethnic foods" in Milwaukee, Wisconsin? A lovely Greek lady took time to write this recipe for me. That's what you call "Greek hospitality."

1 cup water	1 to 2 cups sifted flour
1 package dry yeast	vegetable oil (for deep frying)
1 cup warm milk	2 cups honey
1/4 teaspoon salt	1 cup water
3 eggs, separated	
1 teaspoon vanilla	

Soften yeast in 1 cup warm water. Pour the warm milk into a large bowl; add salt. Stir in yeast, slightly beaten egg yolks, and vanilla; mix well. Add sifted flour, beating continuously until batter is smooth and thick. In a separate mixing bowl beat egg whites with electric beaters until the whites stand in peaks. Fold stiff egg whites into batter. Cover and store batter in a warm place for several hours to let rise.

Pour 3 to 4 inches of cooking oil into deep saucepan and heat until very hot. Blend honey and water thoroughly in a saucepan. Simmer for 5 minutes. Stir the batter well. Drop a tablespoonful of batter into hot oil; cook until the batter puffs and is golden brown on all sides. Remove and drain on paper towel. Place lookoomahthes on a platter in layers, sprinkling each layer lavishly with honey syrup. Makes 30 doughnuts.

Caramel Custard in a Cup (Crema Karamela)

When dining out in Astoria's tavernas, remember to order this wonderful dessert, along with a cup of Greek coffee (kafedaki). It hits the spot!

6 eggs, slightly beaten
3/4 cup sugar (for glaze)
2 cups milk
1/4 cup sugar
1/4 teaspoon salt
1 teaspoon vanilla

Brown 3/4 cup of sugar in bottom of heavy skillet over low flame until caramelized. Pour on bottom of six pyrex cups. Mix 1/4 cup of sugar with milk and scald. Slowly add milk to the slightly beaten eggs. Add the salt and vanilla and stir. Pour in the prepared custard cups. Set cups in pan of water and bake at 350° for about one hour. Refrigerate for an hour or so and turn upside down on a small plate for serving. Makes 6 servings.

Walnut Honeys (Katathes)

1/2 pound butter	1 pound ground walnuts
1 cup oil	3 tablespoons butter, melted
1 teaspoon baking soda	4 tablespoons honey
1 cup water	confectioners' sugar
flour	

Cream butter and oil. Mix baking soda with water. Add flour and soda-water mixture, alternating the two, to butter and oil. Use as much flour as is necessary in order to form a small ball without the dough sticking to your hands. Combine the ground walnuts, butter, and honey for filling. Take one tablespoonful of dough and make a ball. Flatten ball between palms and fill center with 3/4 teaspoon of the nut mixture. Fold dough over to retain mixture and roll to seal. Make into a crescent shape and bake at 350° for 20 minutes. Cover with sifted confectioners' sugar while warm. Yields 50.

Halvah (Halva Tou Fournou)

My cousin, Connie Gekas, from Niles, Illinois, introduced me to this recipe. This is an unusual cake that has no flour in it at all.

1/2 pound butter	Syrup:
1 cup sugar	2 cups sugar
4 eggs	3 cups water
2 cups cream of wheat	1 whole clove
1 teaspoon cinnamon	1 ounce brandy
1 teaspoon baking powder	1 tablespoon lemon juice
1/2 cup almonds, peeled and coarsely chopped	
1 teaspoon vanilla	

Cream butter and add sugar. Slowly add eggs, one at a time, beating well. Add cream of wheat to egg mixture, mixing well. Add cinnamon, baking powder, almonds, and vanilla; blend to form a smooth batter. Pour into a buttered 9 x 13 inch baking pan. Bake in a 350° oven for 30 minutes. To make syrup: combine sugar, water, lemon juice, and clove in a saucepan, bring to a boil, lower heat, and simmer for 10 minutes. Remove from fire and add brandy. Let cool. Serves 12.

Custard Pastry #1 (Galatoboureko)

This is the most popular dessert in Greece, and you'll find it on the menu at most Greek restaurants in New York. It's a traditional favorite for Greek families to prepare Galatoboureko on holidays and special occasions. I'm going to single out this recipe from Stella Pavalatos as my first choice.

2 quarts milk

3 cups sugar

1 cup farina

8 eggs, beaten

$^1/_2$ pound filo

$^1/_2$ pound butter

$1^1/_2$ teaspoons vanilla

Syrup:

    2 cups sugar

    $1^1/_2$ cups water

    thin slice lemon

In a deep pot, heat milk with sugar. Add farina, simmer, uncovered, until thickened, stirring constantly with a wooden spoon. Beat eggs and combine with milk mixture; blend thoroughly. Add vanilla flavoring. Remove from heat and set aside to cool slightly.

Grease 9 x 13 inch baking pan with melted butter. Arrange half the filo in pan, brushing each with melted butter. Pour in farina mixture and top with remaining filo, brushing each with melted butter. Fold edges to retain mixture; brush with melted butter. With a sharp knife, cut through top layers of filo in lengthwise strips. Bake in 350° oven until lightly browned, about 45 minutes.

For syrup, combine ingredients in saucepan and simmer until a medium thick syrup is formed. Cool before pouring over warm pastry. Makes 24 servings.

Custard Pastry #2 (Galatoboureko)

A second version of the popular Greek dessert.

1 quart milk
1/2 cup cream of wheat
1 cup sugar
2 tablespoons butter
1/4 teaspoon salt
6 eggs, well beaten
2 teaspoons vanilla extract
15 filo
3/4 cup butter, melted
Syrup:
  3 cups sugar
  1 1/2 cups water
  2 tablespoons lemon juice

In a deep saucepan, heat milk. Add cream of wheat, sugar, butter, and salt and cook over low heat stirring constantly with a wooden spoon, about 5 minutes. Slowly blend some of the hot milk mixture with the beaten eggs, add vanilla extract, stirring all the while. Combine with mixture in saucepan, and stir over low heat for 2 minutes. Remove from heat and add flavoring.

In a buttered 13 x 9 inch baking pan, arrange 8 buttered filo. Pour in custard mixture and cover with buttered filo. Seal edges, and with sharp knife cut long slits through top filo, about 2 inches apart. Bake at 350° for 35 to 40 minutes.

For syrup, boil ingredients together for 10 minutes. Allow to cool. Pour over warm pastry. Let stand 15 minutes before cutting into diamond-shaped pieces. Makes 30 servings.

Baked Kadaifi Pastry Sheet Style (Kadaifi)

Simple and quick! The large, impressive kadaifi rolls are the more famous method. Walnuts may be mixed with the almonds for a nice variation. Pastries are the standouts at Acropolis Restaurant in Manhattan.

1 pound commercial raw kadaifi pastry

$^1/_2$ cup melted sweet butter

$1^1/_2$ cups blanched finely chopped almonds

$3^1/_2$ cups sugar

4 tablespoons ground cinnamon

$^1/_2$ cup orange juice (optional)

2 cups water

$^1/_2$ cup honey

2 tablespoons lemon juice

Open raw kadaifi pastry and allow to breathe for 10 to 15 minutes. Spread half the pastry evenly over the bottom of a 9 x 12 x 3 inch baking pan and brush with half the butter. Meanwhile, combine the almonds, $^1/_2$ cup sugar, 1 tablespoon cinnamon, and orange juice in a small bowl. (The orange juice will make the mixture like a paste that can be spread with a knife.) Spread the almond mixture over the kadaifi and cover with the remaining pastry. Brush with the remaining butter and bake in a 350° oven for 40 minutes or until golden brown.

In a saucepan, boil the remaining 3 cups of sugar with water for 5 minutes. Stir in honey and lemon juice, bring to a boil, and keep hot. Pour the hot syrup over the pastry. Cover with sheet wax paper and allow to cool. Sprinkle top of pastry with ground cinnamon, and serve. Makes 12 to 14 servings.

Baklava

Baklava is a gala pastry prepared for special occasions: celebrations, holidays, christenings, and weddings.

Follow the scent of almonds and honey, and there you will find Greek sweets. Sweets to a Greek are not restricted to after meals. We like to eat them throughout the day, often accompanied by a strong Greek coffee or a sip of ouzo.

4 cups walnuts

$^{1}/_{2}$ cup ground graham crackers (6 to 8 squares)

2 tablespoons sugar

2 teaspoons cinnamon

1 teaspoon clove powder (optional)

1 pound unsalted butter

1 pound filo (strudel leaves)

Syrup:

    2 cups sugar

    1$^{1}/_{4}$ cups water

    juice of $^{1}/_{2}$ lemon

    $^{1}/_{4}$ cup honey

Chop walnuts coarsely and mix with next four ingredients. Carefully place 8 sheets of filo in a lightly greased 9 x 13 inch pyrex baking dish. The filo should slightly overlap the edge of baking dish. Sprinkle 1 cup of nut mixture evenly over filo leaves. Add 3 more sheets of filo and continue the same process until you have finished with 8 sheets of filo on top, using up all the nut mixture (4 layers of walnut mixture).

Using a sharp knife, cut baklava in diamond-shaped pieces. In a saucepan heat butter until hot (do not burn), and pour hot butter slowly over cut baklava.

In a 350° oven bake until a deep chestnut color, crisp, and baked through, about 45 minutes. Check after 30 minutes to see if baklava is browning evenly; if not, rotate the pan or use tinfoil for remainder of baking. Let cool.

For syrup: In a saucepan, boil sugar and water for 10 minutes. Add honey and lemon juice. Bring back to boil and simmer for 5 minutes. Pour hot syrup over the partially cooled baklava. Baklava should absorb the syrup. Makes 30 servings.

NOTE: After layering and before cutting, tuck in filo neatly all the way around, trim off excess filo, for appearance.

Melomakarona

Vasilenas in Piraeus, Greece, serves an 18 course dinner. You can eat till you pop, but don't. Save some room so you can enjoy this pastry. I happened to meet the baker from this wonderful restaurant while he was visiting New York. He was so thoughtful to write this recipe for my book.

2   sticks butter or margarine
    (room temperature)

$1/2$ cup sugar

2   cups vegetable oil

2   eggs

$1/2$ cup orange juice

rind of 1 orange

1   cordial glass whiskey

1   teaspoon baking soda

2   cups flour

Syrup:

> $1/2$ cup honey
>
> 1   cup sugar
>
> $1^1/4$ cups water

Cream butter, sugar, and oil. Add eggs and continue mixing. Add juice, rind, and whiskey; blend well. Add baking soda to 1 cup of the flour and add to mixture. Add remaining flour, mixing by hand, until dough is soft—mixture must not be sticky and not too stiff. Form as desired into cookies. Bake on ungreased cookie sheet in 350° oven for 15 minutes. To make syrup: Mix honey, sugar, and water. Boil gently for 5 minutes. When cookies are done, dip in honey syrup. Makes 3 dozen cookies.

Melomakarona II

My mother-in-law, Vasilaki Pappas, brought this recipe over from Sparta, Greece, by boat over seventy years ago. She is now deceased, but relatives and friends still continue to enjoy her favorite pastries.

3¼ cups vegetable oil

½ cup sugar

1 egg

1 cup orange juice

9 cups flour

½ teaspoon nutmeg

¼ teaspoon cloves

1 teaspoon cinnamon

1¼ teaspoons baking soda

¼ teaspoon salt

1 ounce brandy

Syrup:

    ½ cup honey

    1 cup sugar

    1¼ cups water

Topping:

    ½ pound nuts, finely ground

    ½ teaspoon cinnamon

    3 tablespoons sugar

With an electric mixer, beat oil and sugar together. Add egg and continue beating. Add orange juice and blend well. Add brandy. Sift flour with nutmeg, cloves, cinnamon, baking soda, and salt. Slowly add flour mixture to sugar, mixing by hand, to form a soft dough. Form small portions of dough into oval shapes, and make indentation with thumb. Place on an ungreased cookie sheet; bake in a 350° oven for 20 minutes, or until golden. Mix syrup ingredients in saucepan and boil gently for 5 minutes. Allow cookies to cool. Dip 4 to 5 cookies in simmering syrup for a few minutes, turning several times. With a slotted spoon, remove cookies and place in a colander to drain slightly. Combine nuts, cinnamon, and sugar and sprinkle over cookies. Makes 4 dozen cookies.

Buttered Cookies (Kourambiethes)

Every child boasts about their mother's cookies being the best. Why should I be any different? Try my mother's favorite recipe.

1 pound sweet butter

$1/4$ cup confectioners' sugar

2 egg yolks

$5 1/4$ cups sifted flour

1 tablespoon vanilla

confectioners' sugar (for sprinkling)

Cream butter, sugar, and egg yolks until light and fluffy. Slowly add sifted flour and mix. Add vanilla flavoring. With your hands, form dough, about $1/2$ tablespoon at a time, into balls, crescents, or S-shapes. Place cookies about 2 inches apart on cookie sheet. Bake in a 350° oven for 20 minutes or until barely brown around the edges. Remove cookies and carefully place on flat surface, which has been sprinkled with confectioners' sugar. Sprinkle confectioners' sugar over top of cookies. Allow to cool. Makes 6 dozen cookies.

Small Easter Biscuits (Koulourakia Lambriatika)

$1/2$ cup butter

1 cup sugar

3 eggs

lemon rind, grated, to taste

$1/2$ cup milk

5 cups flour

1 egg, beaten

almonds, blanched and shredded

Cream butter and add sugar. Beat until light and fluffy. Add eggs one by one, mixing after each egg. Add lemon rind; beat mixture for about 5 minutes. Stir in milk alternately with enough flour to make a soft dough. Form into pencil-sized strips, about 14 inches long. Fold each strip in half and twist. Join ends to form small rings. Arrange on greased baking sheets; brush with egg and sprinkle with almonds. Bake in 350° oven for about 18 minutes.

Sesame seeds can be substituted for almonds. Makes 6 dozen cookies.

Buttered Cookies (Koulourakia Voutirou)

Bertha Dangles contributed several excellent recipes to the St. Nicholas Greek Orthodox Church cookbook. This cookie is a favorite for the young and old. I myself enjoy Koulourakia with a cup of Greek coffee.

1   pound butter

1   cup sugar

1/2 cup vegetable oil

3   eggs

1   jigger whiskey

7   cups flour, sifted

3   teaspoons baking powder

1/4 cup milk

Cream butter with sugar and oil until creamy. Beat in eggs and add whiskey; beat well. Sift flour with baking powder and gradually add to the above mixture, alternately with milk. Remove bowl from mixer and gradually add flour and knead slightly. Mixture must be soft and not too sticky. Form cookies as desired. Sprinkle with sesame seeds. Place on baking sheet and bake at 350° for 20 minutes or until lightly brown. Makes 7 dozen cookies.

Sweet Biscuits I (Paximadia)

Bertha Capulos is the author of this delicious cookie. Thanks, Bertha, for allowing my readers in your kitchen.

1   teaspoon baking powder
    for each cup flour used

2   teaspoons cinnamon

dash of clove powder

8 to 10 cups flour

6   sticks butter, room temperature

1/2 cup corn oil

3   cups sugar

1/2 teaspoon baking soda

1/2 cup milk

6   eggs

sesame seeds (for sprinkling)

Sift baking powder, cinnamon, and clove powder together with flour. Cream butter, add oil and sugar; whip well. Dissolve baking soda in milk and add to butter. Fold in eggs and continue beating. Slowly add the flour. As the mixture thickens, remove from electric mixer and mix by hand, forming a soft dough.

Make one large roll. Divide roll into 8 portions. Roll each portion to the length of a cookie sheet. Place 2 rolls on a cookie sheet 2 inches apart. Flatten top slightly and sprinkle with sesame seeds. Score top where you will later cut.

Bake in a 350° oven until lightly brown. Remove from oven and slice. Turn slices on their sides. Return to oven and continue to bake until lightly brown. Makes 10 dozen.

Sweet Biscuits II (Paximadia)

Thanks to my sister-in-law, Mary Pappas, for her award winning recipe. I'm sure everyone that makes this recipe will want to express their thanks to Mary, too.

3/4 cup butter

3/4 cup sugar

3 eggs, beaten

1/2 cup almonds, chopped

2 1/2 cups flour

1/2 tablespoon baking powder

1 teaspoon baking soda

1 tablespoon salad oil

Cream butter, and beat in sugar gradually. Beat in eggs and nuts. Sift dry ingredients together and blend with butter mixture gradually. Add salad oil. Shape into 3 loaves about 1 inch thick. Place loaves on a baking sheet and bake at 350° for 30 minutes or until lightly brown. Remove from oven and slice. Turn slices on their sides. Return to oven and continue to bake for 30 minutes longer or until lightly brown. Makes 48 biscuits.

Ravani Cake (Ravani)

This smoothly flowing cake is best made well in advance to give the flavors a chance to permeate the ravani.

Olga Gekas, my cousin, supplied this formula that produces a pleasantly sweet, subtly spiced cake.

1 cup butter

1 cup sugar

6 eggs, separated

2 cups milk

2 cups farina

2 cups flour

4 teaspoons baking powder

3 teaspoons salt

1 teaspoon vanilla

1 cup almonds, blanched and chopped

2 cups sugar

2 cups water

cinnamon (for sprinkling)

Cream butter with 1 cup sugar until very light. Add egg yolks and continue beating. Add milk and farina. Sift flour with baking powder and salt; add to butter mixture along with vanilla and almonds. Mix well.

In another bowl, beat the egg whites until stiff. Fold them into the batter. Pour into a greased 9 x 13 inch pan. Spread evenly and bake in a 350° oven until golden, about 45 minutes.

While cake is baking, in a saucepan combine 2 cups sugar with the water and bring to boil. Simmer for 5 minutes. As soon as cake is removed from oven, pour hot syrup over cake. Let cool. Just before serving, sprinkle cinnamon over top. Serves 24.

Rice Pudding (Rizogalo)

Greeks may not have invented this delicious creamy dessert, but they did invent a name for it. We Greeks call it rizogalo (which means "rice milk"). Enjoy!

3/4 cup rice

1 quart milk

2 cups water

1 cup sugar

dash of salt

1 teaspoon vanilla

cinnamon for topping

Place rice in bowl of warm water to soften. Rub rice between your palms to crush grains to size of tapioca. Drain.

In a deep saucepan, bring milk and water to a boil. Stir in crushed rice, sugar, and dash of salt. Cook over moderate heat, stirring occasionally, until rice is cooked and mixture has thickened, about 40 minutes. Remove from heat and add vanilla. Pour into individual dishes; sprinkle with cinnamon. Makes 8 servings.

Baked Apples With Honey Syrup (Mila Tou Fournou)

This simple, but delicious, baked apple recipe was Mom Gekas' morning chore at Dad's restaurant.

4 medium cooking apples	1 cup water
1/2 cup walnuts, chopped	1/2 cup sugar
1/4 cup golden raisins	1/2 cup honey
1 teaspoon sugar	1 teaspoon lemon juice
1/2 teaspoon ground cinnamon	1 cinnamon stick
1/4 teaspoon ground cloves	whipped cream

Core apples, being careful not to cut through the bottom. Pare 1/2 inch at the stem end.

Combine walnuts, raisins, 1 teaspoon sugar, ground cinnamon, and cloves. Fill the center of the apples with the mixture. Place apples in a 8 x 8 inch baking pan. Set aside.

In a saucepan, combine water, 1/2 cup sugar, honey, lemon juice, and cinnamon stick and bring to a boil. Simmer for 2 minutes. Pour mixture over apples. Bake in 375° oven until tender, about 45 minutes, basting occasionally with syrup from the pan.

Serve warm or let cool, chill, and serve cold. Accompany apples with whipped cream. Makes 4 servings.

Walnut Syrup Sponge Cake (Karidopita)

Syrup cake is a traditional Greek favorite. This is one of the richer versions, which can be made in advance and served in small portions at tea or a buffet.

3 cups water	1 teaspoon vanilla
4 cups sugar	1/2 teaspoon baking soda
peel of 1 orange	1 (6-ounce) package zwieback, crushed fine
2 cloves	
18 eggs, separated	4 cups walnuts, coarsely chopped
5 tablespoons cognac	1 teaspoon ground cinnamon

Combine water, 2 1/2 cups of sugar, orange peel, and cloves in a saucepan; boil for 10 minutes. Remove orange peel and cloves and allow mixture to cool.

Meanwhile, using an electric mixer, beat egg yolks until light. Continue beating and gradually add the remaining 1 1/2 cups of sugar.

In a separate bowl, mix the cognac, vanilla, and baking soda and slowly add to yolks and sugar. Combine zwieback, walnuts, and cinnamon. Gradually add to batter, mixing on low speed. Beat egg whites until soft peaks form. Slowly fold into cake batter, then pour into greased 15 1/2 x 11 x 2 inch baking pan. Bake in a 350° oven for 30 minutes, or until a deep chestnut color. Remove from the oven and set on a wire rack. Spoon the cooled syrup over the cake and allow cake to cool in the pan. Cut into traditional diamond shapes. Makes 20 to 24 servings.

Greek Pecan Cake (Karthopita)

1/2 pound butter, softened	1 teaspoon cinnamon
1 cup sugar	1 teaspoon grated orange peel
5 eggs, large	Syrup:
1 cup flour, sifted	3 cups water
1 cup farina	2 cups sugar
1 cup finely chopped pecans	1/2 teaspoon cinnamon
2 teaspoons baking powder	1 slice lemon

In a large bowl, cream butter and sugar until light; add eggs, one at a time, beating constantly. Add flour, farina, baking powder, cinnamon, and orange peel; beat well. Add finely chopped pecans and mix thoroughly. Pour batter into a 9 x 13 inch buttered cookie sheet, and bake in a 350° oven for 35 minutes.

For syrup combine all ingredients in a saucepan, boil 10 minutes. Set aside and cool. Pour cooled syrup over cake and allow to cool. Cut cake into diamond shapes. Makes 24 servings.

Greek Orange Cake

The Taverna Delphi near Syntagma Square in Athens has excellent food, along with the best pastries.

1 stick butter	1 teaspoon baking soda
1 cup sugar	1 small package skinned and chopped almonds
1/2 pint sour cream	
juice and rind of 1 orange	Syrup:
3 eggs, well beaten	3/4 cup sugar
2 cups cake flour	1/2 cup water
1 teaspoon baking powder	

Cream together butter and sugar. Add sour cream, orange juice, and rind; mix well. Add beaten eggs and blend well. Sift dry ingredients together and add to above mixture. Fold in chopped almonds. Pour batter into buttered round 12 x 12 inch pan. Bake at 350° for approximately 1 hour. For syrup, combine sugar and water. Simmer for 5 minutes; let cool. Remove cake from oven and immediately pour cool syrup over hot cake. When cake cools, cut into diamond shapes. Makes 10 servings.

Athens Pecan Cake

This recipe is a big hit at the Taverna Anna Restaurant in North Filotheh, a suburb of Athens. If you like pecans, you'll enjoy this cake.

$^1/_2$ pound butter

1 cup sugar

6 eggs, well beaten

rind of 1 orange

1 cup chopped pecans

$^1/_2$ ounce brandy

2 cups flour

4 teaspoons baking powder

Cream butter and sugar. Fold in beaten eggs and blend well. Add orange rind, nuts, and brandy and mix well. Add flour and baking powder, blending thoroughly. Pour into a greased 9 x 13 inch baking sheet. Bake in a 350° oven for 40 minutes, or until done. Makes 24 servings.

Honey Cheese Pie (Melopita)

I'm the creator of this recipe. So simple to make—you're going to enjoy this one.

4 eggs, slightly beaten

2 cups ricotta cheese

1 cup honey

$^1/_2$ teaspoon cinnamon

2 tablespoons flour

1 teaspoon lemon juice

cinnamon (for sprinkling)

Beat eggs lightly in a large mixing bowl. Add ricotta cheese, honey, cinnamon, flour, and lemon juice. Beat for 3 minutes or until very smooth. Brush a tablespoon of melted butter in a 9-inch pie pan; pour in mixture. Bake in 350° oven for 1 hour, or until done. Remove from oven and sprinkle with cinnamon. Let cool before cutting. Makes 8 servings.

Grecian Creme

Forget counting calories when it comes to enjoying this wonderful dessert.

1 package raspberry gelatin (3 ounces)
1/4 teaspoon salt
1 cup boiling water
1/4 cup cold water
2 teaspoons lemon juice

1/3 cup honey
1/2 cup light cream
1/2 cup chopped pecans
whipped topping

Dissolve gelatin and salt in boiling water. Stir in cold water, lemon juice, and honey. Chill until slightly thickened by placing bowl in a larger bowl filled with ice and water. Beat with an electric hand mixer until fluffy and thick (double in volume). Gently stir in cream and nuts. Spoon into a 1-quart mold. When ready to serve, remove from mold and garnish with whipped topping, more pecans, and a light drizzle of honey. Makes 6 to 8 servings.

Yogurt Cake (Yiaourtopita)

1 cup butter
1 1/2 cups sugar
3 eggs
1 cup yogurt
1 teaspoon grated lemon peel
1 teaspoon vanilla
1 teaspoon cinnamon
2 1/2 cups flour
2 teaspoons baking powder
1 teaspoon baking soda
1/2 teaspoon salt
1 cup almonds, blanched and chopped

Cream butter with sugar. Add eggs and beat until fluffy. Add yogurt, lemon peel, vanilla, and cinnamon. Sift flour with baking powder, baking soda, and salt. Add to mixture and blend well. Fold in almonds. Pour into a greased 9 x 13 inch baking pan. Bake in a 350° oven for 55 minutes, or until chestnut color. Makes 14 servings.

"And lately, by the Tavern door agape,
Came shining through the Dusk an Angel Shape
Bearing a Vessel on his Shoulder; and
He bid me taste of it; and 'twas—the Grape!"

"Then to the lip of this poor earthern Urn
I lean'd, the Secret of my Life to learn:
And Lip to Lip it murmur'd—"While you live
Drink!—for once dead you never shall return."

"A Book of Verses underneath the Bough,
A Jug of Wine, a Loaf of Bread—and Thou
Beside me singing in the Wilderness—
Oh, Wilderness were Paradise enow!"

from *The Rubaiyat* of Omar Khayyam

WINE &
BEVERAGES

Greek Wines

Greece has many excellent wines but the most popular wine is Retsina. Because of the resin used to give it its subtle aroma and flavor, some say it tastes like turpentine. Retsina has been found in wrecked ships at the bottom of the Aegean and Mediterranean seas, sealed in ancient amphora, thousands of years old. The ancient Greeks used pitch from the pine covered slopes of Mount Olympus to line these pots and to prevent the jars from sweating and spoiling the wine. Even though it is no longer stored in terra cotta containers, the wine is still flavored with pitch by simply putting a pine cone filled with resin into the vat. Retsina wine is best served chilled, and can be served with any Greek food.

Look for these Greek wines in liquor stores or wine shops.

Wine Selections

RED	**WHITE**	**ROSE**
Mt. Ambelos (dry)	Boutari Retsina (resinated)	Boutari Roditis
Cava Tsantalis	Cambas Retsina (resinated)	Cambas Roditis
Demestica (dry)	Mt. Ambelos (dry)	Calliga Rose
Boutari Naoussa (dry)	Demestica (dry)	
Mavrodaphine (sweet)	Santa Elena (dry)	
Grande Reserve Boutari (dry)	Boutari Blanc (dry)	
Chateau Carras	Patsras Cavino (dry)	
Calliga Ruby	Makedonikos Tsantalis	
Cava Calliga	Agioritikos Tsantalis	
	Chateau Matsa, Boutari (dry)	

Lemonade (Lemonada)

1   cup lemon juice (8 ounces)

2   cups sugar

6   cups ice water

In a glass pitcher, combine lemon juice, sugar, and water. Stir until the sugar is dissolved. Serve in glasses with a slice of lemon or mint. Makes 6 servings.

Greek Coffee

Greek coffee is served after dinner, often with a glass of cognac. It is made in a small, brass coffeemaker and served in demitasse cups. Greek coffee is extremely strong and is meant for leisurely sipping. The sign of a well-made cup is the foam floating on the top of the coffee.

4 demitasse cups of cold water

long-handled, brass, 4-cup Greek coffeemaker

4 level teaspoons sugar

4 rounded teaspoons Turkish coffee

Pour 4 demitasse cups of cold water into coffeemaker. Bring to a boil. Add sugar; stir until dissolved. Maintain boiling temperature. Add coffee, stirring well. Remove coffeemaker immediately from heat. A foam should appear on the surface of the coffee. Pour a little of this foam evenly into each of the 4 demitasse cups. Then, carefully fill the cups with the remaining coffee. Serve immediately. To gain Greek coffee's full flavor, sip slowly and allow the fine, thick grounds to settle to the bottom of the cup. Sip until you reach the grounds.

Greek Egg Nog

1 egg, beaten well

3 teaspoons sugar

1/4 teaspoon vanilla

1 glass hot milk

dash of nutmeg

Beat egg, sugar, and vanilla until thick. Add hot milk, and stir well. Sprinkle with nutmeg. Yields 2 cups.

Grecian Hot Chocolate

2 heaping teaspoons cocoa

1 tablespoon sugar

1/2 teaspoon vanilla

8 ounces hot milk

dash of cinnamon

Place cocoa in cup, and add sugar, hot milk, and vanilla. Stir well. Sprinkle with cinnamon. Yields 2 cups.

Coffee Frappe

Omonia Square in Athens serves this wonderful coffee drink. They call it a frappe, and it is served in tall glasses. You can make this frappe in your own kitchen.

Make some espresso coffee and chill it. In a food blender add 1 cup of whole milk, 2 teaspoons whipping cream, and whip it a few seconds, add coffee to taste, along with a bit of sugar, and whip again. Serve in a tall chilled glass.

Glossary of Common Cooking Terms

Bake: Cook, covered or uncovered, with dry heat in an enclosed area such as an oven or closed grill.

Baked blind: Bake a pie crust or tart shell without a filling.

Baste: Drizzle or brush liquid over a food during roasting to keep it moist and/or add flavor.

Beat: Stir rapidly in a lifting motion with a spoon (the same motion with a whisk is called whisking) or mix with a mixer. Beating adds air for lightness.

Blanch: Drop food in boiling water briefly to precook slightly or to loosen skin of a fruit or vegetable for easier peeling.

Blend: Mix thoroughly.

Boil: Cook liquid at a temperature that makes bubbles constantly break on the surface. A rolling boil is a more vigorous boil across the whole surface.

Bone: Remove bones from meat or fish.

Braise: Cook slowly in a small amount of liquid, usually in a frying pan, and often first browned in a little fat.

Bread: Coat with bread or cracker crumbs. When food is dry, it is first coated with egg or milk so crumbs will adhere.

Broil: Cook by dry direct heat either in a broiler or over charcoal.

Brown: Cook in a small amount of fat until surface turns golden brown.

Caramelize: Liquefy sugar over low heat until it turns golden brown.

Chill: Refrigerate or cool over ice water.

Chop: Cut food into small pieces on a cutting board or process to small pieces in a food processor or chopper.

Coat: Cover food surface with some other ingredient such as crumbs or egg.

Coat a spoon: The stage of cooking when a thin coating remains on a metal spoon rather than running off. Often used with custards.

Combine: Stir just until mixed evenly.

Core: Remove seed and hard material from interior of fruit or vegetable.

Cube: Cut into small squares, usually about 1/2 inch. Cubed meat has been scored to break the fibers on the surface to tenderize it.

Cut in: Cut fat with a pastry blender or one or two knives into flour or a flour mixture. Used to make biscuits and pie crust as well as crumb toppings.

Deglaze: Liquefy cooked bits left in the pan after roasting or frying by stirring in stock, wine, or other liquid so it can be used in sauce.

Degrease: Remove fat from surface of a liquid.

Dice: Cut into small pieces, about 1/8 inch to 1/4 inch. Diced food is smaller than cubed.

Dollop: A small mound.

Dot: Sprinkle. Used frequently with butter or cheese on the surface of a pie filling or a casserole.

Dredge: Coat thoroughly either by turning meat, fish, or vegetable in flour or crumbs or by shaking them in a bag.

Drizzle: Pour liquid in a stream. Frosting drizzled on a cake is usually left in a pattern rather than smoothed out.

Dust: Sprinkle lightly (usually with flour or sugar), shaking off small pieces, as with fish.

Flute: Make a decorative wavy edge on pastry.

Fold In: Using a spoon or, preferably, a rubber spatula, gently combine whipped eggs, cream, or other airy food with another food. Cut down with side of spatula through the center of the mixtures to be combined (cut heavier into lighter). Move across the bottom of the container and bring spatula back up, folding heavier mixture from the bottom over the surface. Repeat, turning the bowl with each stroke to distribute evenly.

Fry: Cook in fat. Pan frying cooks in just enough fat to keep food from sticking (the same as sauteing). Deep- (or french-) frying cooks in enough fat to cover the food or allow it to float.

Garnish: Decorate.

Gel: Congeal or become stiff, as in gelatin. Jel has a slightly different consistency and refers to jelly.

Grate: Rub against sharp teeth on a metal or porcelain grater to produce shreds or tiny particles.

Glaze: Coat with a thin icing or gelatinous substance to make shiny.

Grease: Rub with fat or oil. Pans for baking yeast bread should be greased with solid shortening.

Grill: Cook on a rack over coals or cook on a griddle with little, if any, fat.

Hull: Remove stems and leaves.

Julienne: Make matchstick-size pieces.

Knead: Work dough by repeated pushing, folding, and turning to develop the protein (gluten) and give structure to bread and rolls. Dough will become smooth and elastic. Yeast bread takes 15 or 20 minutes to knead; biscuits take about six foldings and a gentler touch. Yeast dough can be kneaded with a dough hook on a heavy-duty mixer.

Marinate: Soak in a spicy or aromatic mixture (marinade).

Mash: Crush to a soft mixture, using a spoon or masher made from metal wire or a piece of metal with holes. Years ago mashers were wooden.

Mince: Cut or chop into very small pieces.

Pan-broil: Cook in a heavy ungreased (or lightly greased) frying pan.

Pot-roast: Cook a large cut of meat in a little liquid, usually after browning. Braise usually refers to small cuts—cubes or slices—but is the same process.

Punch down: Use a fist to push down on yeast dough, then fold over sides and push again to remove air.

Puree: Push through a sieve (strainer) or process in a blender or food processor until smooth.

Reduce: Boil down liquid in an uncovered pan so some of it boils off as steam and the quantity is reduced.

Refresh: Take cooked food from heat and place in a container of cold water to quickly halt cooking.

Roast: Cook uncovered in dry heat in the oven or a covered grill. "Roast" is the term usually used for meats, "bake" for breads and cakes.

Roux: A mixture of fat and flour, cooked to remove raw starch taste, then used to thicken soups, stews, and gravies. The proportion of 2 tablespoons fat and 2 tablespoons flour will thicken 1 cup liquid to gravy consistency.

Scald: Heat to just below the boiling point. Tiny bubbles appear around the edge of the liquid. Often used for milk to be incorporated into a bread recipe.

Sear: Use high heat to quickly brown surface of meat.

Score: Cut through surface layer of meat to tenderize, decorate and/or keep from curling.

Shred: Cut or pull into irregular small pieces, using grater or fork.

Simmer: Cook at low heat just below the boiling point. Bubbles form slowly and break under the surface.

Skim: Remove the top layer of fat or scum from soup or a sauce with a spoon.

Steam: Cook on a rack or in a bowl above the surface of boiling liquid.

Stew: Cook at a simmer in liquid that covers the meat and/or vegetables.

Stir: Use a spoon or whisk in a large circular motion to mix or keep from sticking. Stirring, as opposed to beating, doesn't involve incorporating air into the mixture.

Stir-fry: Cook (frequently in a wok) with continuous stirring in a little fat over high heat.

Toss: Using two forks or spoons, mix ingredients (or coat with dressing) by lifting food into the air and letting it fall back into the bowl.

Truss: Tie the legs of a chicken or other poultry and bend the wings behind the back so bird will hold its shape during cooking.

Whip: Beat with a mixer, wire whip, or whisk to incorporate air and increase the volume of liquid or, as in the case of cream or egg whites, turn it into a fluffy solid.

Zest: The thin outer surface or colored portion of the peel of the citrus fruit. It doesn't include the bitter pithy white portion.

Substitutes

When you're out of an ingredient, improvise.

1 tablespoon cornstarch (for thickening) = 2 tablespoons all-purpose flour.

1 teaspoon baking powder = $1/2$ teaspoon cream of tartar plus $1/4$ teaspoon baking soda.

1 cup sugar = 1 cup packed brown sugar or 2 cups sifted powdered sugar.

1 cup molasses = 1 cup honey.

1 square (1 ounce) unsweetened chocolate = 3 tablespoons unsweetened cocoa powder plus 1 tablespoon shortening or cooking oil, or 1-ounce envelope premelted unsweetened chocolate product.

6 squares (6 ounces) semisweet chocolate = 1 6-ounce package semisweet chocolate pieces, or 6 tablespoons unsweetened cocoa powder plus $1/4$ cup sugar and $1/4$ cup shortening.

1 cup whole milk = $1/2$ cup evaporated milk plus $1/2$ cup water, or 1 cup water plus $1/3$ cup nonfat dry milk powder.

1 cup buttermilk = 1 tablespoon lemon juice or vinegar plus enough milk to make 1 cup (let stand 5 minutes before using) or 1 cup plain yogurt.

1 cup light cream = 1 tablespoon melted butter plus enough milk to make 1 cup.

$1/2$ cup liquor (rum, bourbon, or whiskey) = $1/4$ cup unsweetened fruit juice or both.

$1/2$ cup wine = $1/2$ cup apple or white grape juice (for white wine), or $1/2$ cup unsweetened grape juice (for red wine). Taste recipe before sweetening; you may need less sugar.

1 small onion, chopped = 1 teaspoon onion powder, or 1 tablespoon dried minced onion.

1 tablespoon prepared mustard = $1/2$ teaspoon dry mustard plus 2 teaspoons vinegar.

$1/4$ cup fine dry bread crumbs = $3/4$ cup soft bread crumbs.

Common Food Weights and Measurements

Dash: Less than $1/8$ teaspoon

1 tablespoon: 3 teaspoons

4 tablespoons: $1/4$ cup

$5 1/3$ tablespoons: $1/3$ cup

8 tablespoons: $1/2$ cup

$10 2/3$ tablespoons: $2/3$ cup

12 tablespoons: $3/4$ cup

16 tablespoons: 1 cup

1 fluid ounce: 2 tablespoons

1 cup: $1/2$ pint (liquid)

2 cups: 1 pint

2 pints (4 cups): 1 quart

4 quarts: 1 gallon

8 quarts: 1 peck (dry)

4 pecks: 1 bushel

16 ounces: 1 pound

Oven Temperatures:

I cannot over emphasize the need for correct oven temperature. For optimum results, you need to follow the temperatures indicated in the recipe. Plenty of dishes have been ruined because the oven temperature was not correct.

Temperature (Degree F)	Term
250 to 275	Very Low
300 to 325	Low
350 to 375	Moderate
400 to 425	Hot
450 to 475	Very Hot
500 to 525	Extremely Hot

Index

Author

To most boys growing up means sandlot baseball, skinnydipping on hot summer afternoons, learning to tell the difference between late model cars.

Coming of age was all these things and a whole lot more to George. The big difference in George's rearing and that of the average youngster was his last name—Gekas.

It's as Greek as the Acropolis.

Anyone who knows anything about Greek Americans, knows a good many of them have been exceptionally successful in the hospitality field—mostly in the art of good eating,

And so it was natural for George to be introduced to the business at the age of 12. He was just about old enough to jerk sodas.

His boss, of course, was his father, James Gekas, then executive chef at Gekas Brothers restaurants in Michigan's upper peninsula.

During his early years, George learned every job, from bussing tables to waiting on them, to preparing haute cuisine to running a chain of his own restaurants, including the catering manager of the prestigious Illinois Athletic Club. And later he became general manager of the world renowned Chicago Press Club, a favorite of newspaper and magazine writers and editors, and T.V., radio, sports, and entertainment personalities.

After writing the "Hospitality Career" course in restaurant management, it seemed like the appropriate time to write a cookbook.

This is one of the few cookbooks that begins to describe true Greek cuisine and its secrets. "I thought it proper, therefore, that the gap should be filled, and so I felt that with the zeal and enthusiasm that I experience, I should incorporate practical, contemporary cooking and preparation methods. Thus, my cooking always centered around Greek food. That's where my palate feels at home."

What's most interesting about this book is how a dish will change from one section of the country to another. The basic ingredients remain the same, but the seasonings vary.

This cookbook is a compilation of the best dishes from the finest Greek restaurants of "New York" relatives and friends. These are "top shelf recipes" that alone may be worth the price of the book.

Today George Gekas lives in Chicago with his wife, Helen. George plans on continuing writing, since he has now retired from the hospitality industry, where he spent over 50 years trying to please patrons of all ethnic groups. George has satisfied guests from coast to coast.

OPAA!

FREE Glass of Wine with the Purchase of an Entree at These Restaurants
(Coupons Void if Removed from Book)

Please show the coupon to your server. You and your companions will receive one **FREE** glass of wine with each entree ordered. Not valid with any other discount offers or coupons. Coupons are void if removed from the book. Offer good any day but Friday, Saturday, and holidays.

Taverna Vraka
23–15 31st St.
Astoria, NY

New Acropolis
767 W. 19th Ave. at 47th St.
New York, NY

Estia
308 East 86th Street
New York, NY